Five years ago, experimental writers Roc Sandford and Susana Medina met at the Extinction Rebellion climate protests which were enthralling and irritating people all over the world. *Rebel, Rebel, An Emergency Dialogue* is a street-level account of those days, a blazing call to help protect our planet from the disasters being cooked up for it, and a collage or 'pastiche' of different sorts of writing (dialogue, erotic fable, emails, poetry, texting, short stories, essays). A historical snapshot of Extinction Rebellion in 2019 and 2020, it is an intellectual exposition, an act of planetary defence which registers the life of a rebel family and the new friendship of two rebels, and a literary experiment scattered with references to Dante, Cervantes, Baudelaire, Kafka, Benjamin, Camus, Szymborska, Ballard, Atwood, Callenbach, Gablik, Gosh and others.

ROC SANDFORD is a writer, artist and member of artists' collective *Ocean Rebellion*. Roc modelled perceptual bias at Bristol, Penn State, and UCL and is a director of Mathematical Sciences UK, David Graeber Institute and Absurd Intelligence. They present a message of climate and nature collapse, currently inadequate policy response and sector-specific asks to multilateral bodies, finance, accountancy, government and academia. Writing, editing and interviews have appeared in many major print and broadcast channels and numerous documentaries have featured Roc's work. Their most recent book, *Burnt Rain* (Hazel Press) was published in July 2023. www.rocsandford.com

SUSANA MEDINA is the author of *Philosophical Toys*, offspring of which are the short films *Buñuel's Philosophical Toys* and *Leather-bound Stories* (co-directed with Derek Ogbourne); *Red Tales* (bilingual ed. co-translated with Rosie Marteau); and *Souvenirs del Accidente*. Her story 'Oestrogen' was published in *Best European Fiction, 2014* (Dalkey Archive Press). She has been awarded the Max Aub Short Story International Prize and an ACE Writing Grant for *Spinning Days of Night*, forthcoming in 2024.

She is a climate activist, taking action and appearing on stages for Extinction Rebellion UK, including the legendary pink boat at Oxford Circus, Edinburgh Fringe and Writers Rebel's 40 Top Writers Marathon. www.susanamedina.net

Rebel, Rebel

Carboniferous Forest by Robert Gibbings

REBEL, REBEL

An Emergency Dialogue

Roc Sandford &
Susana Medina

GOMETRA

First published in June 2024 by
Gometra Press, Isle of Gometra,
Ulva Ferry, Isle of Mull, PA73 6NA
www.gometra.org

Third edition November 2025

All rights reserved. No part of this publication may be
reproduced in any form or by any means
without the prior permission of the publisher.

A CIP record for this title is available from the British Library

Frontispiece and title page recto
wood engravings © Robert Gibbings
Text © Susana Medina 2024 and
© Roc Sandford 2024 respectively
Set in Eric Gill's *Golden Cockerel*
in 48, 24, 20, 12, 11 & 9 point fonts
by Roc Sandford
Cover design by This Ain't Rock'n'Roll
Version dated 16/11/25
Printed & bound in England in
Royal Octavo by IngramSpark

Cloth ISBN 978-1-906180-13-3
Paperback ISBN 978-1-906180-31-7

Gometra # 25 & 38

Contents

Chicxulub Asteroid—1
  The Possibility of Denial—2

May 2019 Emails: Super-Highway to Rebellion—7
  Dear Angelus Novus—8

May 2019 Dialogue: Paolozzi Rendezvous—19

Paolozzi Rendezvous—21
  Art of Digression—21
  Tragedy, Humour, Clarity—27
  Naked Rebels in Parliament—28
  What Children Know—30

Re: Easter Rebellion, 2019—33
  Rebel Rebel—33
  Do No Harm—36
  Reforesting the Mind—39
  Becoming Ecological Humans—40
  Polluter Pays or Polluter Steals—44
  The Problem of Evil: Rampant Consumerism—46
  Volcanic: Twenty Nineteen—48

Degrowth of Damage—51
  Fossil Fuels Inferno—51
  Chronicle of Climate Chaos Foretold ... by ExxonMobil—52

    Science and Humanity Divide—55

    Frugality, Cats and Utopia—57

    Costa Rica, Cuba, Bolivia and Ecuador Lead the Way—58

    NIMBY & the Disconnect of City Cultures—60

    Degrowth of Damage—62

    Zero Sum Game—64

June 2019 Dialogue: Ratatouille Rendezvous—67

Ratatouille Rendezvous—69

    Carbon's Dividend and the Problem of Evil—69

    Ecocide—72

    Gandhi & Urgent Transitions—74

    Rationing, Recycling & the Dismal Fashion Industry—76

    Climate Chaos: a Unifying Force—77

    Slavery, Colonialism and Climate Change—77

Waterloo Bridge: It Was Very, Very Wonderful—85

    Non-Violent Direct Action—85

    Evil fights Back—86

    Declaration of Climate Emergency—88

    Minitrue—89

    Plato's Guardians—91

    It was Very, Very Wonderful—93

    Propaganda Model—101

    The End is Nigh—101

    New Reality Calls for New Stories—103

July 2019 Emails: Codename Project Mushroom—105

    Thursday 19 July: The Polly Higgins Boat, a Texting Interlude—110

    Moby Dickery—111

August 2019 Emails: Dear Angelus Novus—117

December 2019 Emails: The October Rebellion—131
   October Rebellion—131

Goodbye, Pink Cushions & Disability Toilets: The October Rebellion—149
   Overture—149
   Trafalgar Sq Rhapsody—150

January 2020: The Tragic Mountain, or The Four Planes of Davos—163
   Dark Wood—163
   Purgatorio—166
   Inferno—168
   Paradiso—172

The Emotional Alphabet Children—175

September 2020: On Edge, The September Rebellion—187

2024 Coda—191
   Afterword—191

Addendum—193
   Susana's Postscript: From Writing Rebellion, with Love, June 2021—193
   From Writing Rebellion with Love—194

Acknowledgments—205

Stories

Dear Angelus Novus, Susana Medina—8

Siege of the Byzantines, Roc Sandford—118

To Milk a Unicorn, Roc Sandford—139

Trafalgar Sq Rhapsody, Susana Medina—150

The Tragic Mountain, *or* The Four Planes of Davos, Roc Sandford—163

The Emotional Alphabet Children, Susana Medina—175

To the dead of climate and nature collapse.

And to the brave and ingenious rebels, all over the world, who are doing their best to save the rest of us.

This book was written between 2019 and 2021. We were full of hope, perhaps misplaced.

We'll know soon enough.

Chicxulub Asteroid

> The point about hope is that it is something that occurs in very dark moments. It is like a flame in the darkness; it isn't like a confidence and a promise. *John Berger*

Once upon a time, there was a celestial body at least six miles in diameter. Travelling at roughly 13 miles per second, it hit the earth at an angle of just under 60 degrees, a few miles from present day Chicxulub on the Yucatán peninsula. This was the Cretaceous–Paleogene extinction event which, creating a nuclear winter and acidifying the oceans, annihilated the non-avian dinosaurs and countless other species.

Sixty-six million years later, knowing we too were on course to become an asteroid which would create a nuclear summer, that we, like hundreds of species, could become extinct, but also had countermeasures, millions of us across the globe have answered in different ways the burning call to protect the earth and ourselves. To document our civic duty to disobey, Roc and I began a dialogue about one of these ways: Extinction Rebellion, also known as XR, first by email and then recordings. Originally meant as an interview for 3:*AM Magazine*, it soon degenerated into a collage or pastiche of different sorts of writing, a historical snapshot, literary experiment, intellectual exposition, and act of planetary defence.

We started it one month after the 2019 Easter Rebellion, as ordinary rebels who'd been along for the ride. Rooted in a moment already receding into the past, it covers the momentous months which opened a national conversation about ecological chaos. The disaster story wasn't new; for decades our planet threw at us an avalanche of alarming facts, and cautioned us we can thrive without harming it. but the visionaries had been muted. It showed us its unequivocally wounded landscapes, haunted by wildlife hunted to extinction, which filled the air with loss and ghosts. It kept telling us this is a horror story, with predators and prey, while stressing the sacred flaws in stories about civilisation and modernity we had been deceiving ourselves with. It kept pointing out that the myth of progress is the reality we had been hallucinating, and that we were accelerating towards catastrophe. Recently, it started spelling out its wounded story with unprecedented, record-breaking wildfires and heat, flash floods, storms, melting glaciers and drought. And so the Overton window began to open on possibility. A new structure of feeling emerged, yet corporate headquarters keep on sending out-of-office replies.

Our planet keeps telling us who we are and who we need to become. It keeps spitting out bewildering data about collapsing ecosystems, and extreme weather events which are happening much earlier and faster than in the predictions. It keeps warning us what to expect if we don't act. And this year, it has sent us another plot line to its wounded story: degraded ecosystems equal viruses and pandemics. The moral being that the best vaccine is a healthy nature. With a second lockdown in sight, eagerly awaiting both vaccines, while wondering what to write for this introduction, I asked Roc to email me his ideas. He sent me this:

The Possibility of Denial

> Symptoms of ruin. Vast Pelasgic buildings, one on top of the other. Apartments, rooms, temples, galleries, stairways, caeca, belvederes, lanterns, fountains, statues. – Fissures and cracks. Dampness resulting from a reservoir situated near the sky. – How to warn people and nations? Let us whisper warnings into the ears of the most intelligent. *Charles Baudelaire*

Why is the world sinking, flooding, burning? Why is nature dying?

Because, along with almost everybody else, the storytellers have failed.

We're telling the scariest story ever—the human sacrifice, on the altar of facile consumerism, of our own children.

But even when we imagine we are heard, people just carry on, busy with their child-torture—the flights, the cruises, the Amazon-burgers.

We cry apocalypse, and apocalypse has come. Elsewhere, people are torched and gasping. We may or may not be next, but *our* children are.

Yet complacency is unmoved. As storytellers, as humans, as parents, we are not getting through. Dial 999 if you must, but nobody picks up.

How to get people to hear—that's the project—when nobody wants to hear, because if we hear we will either have to admit we don't love our children—or else that we do, but we love our cars, our meat, our air conditioning more.

We may not care about other people's children, but do we or don't we care about our own? It's crunch time.

> The glee he was said to feel in eating walnuts, when he would imagine he was crunching the brains of children. *Levallois on Baudelaire*

When I speak to people out on the streets, there are three main gambits—to deny there is an emergency, to deny they have any power, or to say it is too late. A variant is 'What about China?' If others are going to torch climate and nature, why can't I?

Sometimes, having spoken, they will scratch vigorously in the corners of their eyes before inspecting their fingertips. So what is the spell which will wake these sleeping beauties? Is it a simple kiss? On guilty lips, with their imperceptible breathing, open just enough to disclose a greyish-yellow glint of teeth? Where are the magic words which will puncture their denial? Will these words be fiction, reportage, journalism, polemic, something poly-stylistic? A plea for mercy by the children themselves? A spirited and visionary refusal of the invitation to mount the steps of the scaffold by these under-age and quaking Scheherezades wishing, understandably, to keep the executioner with the ridiculous cap, the sweaty belly and the mechanical slicer waiting?

Because somewhere lurks a sacred text which melts the frozen hearts of those notorious child-killers, you and me. Which, teaching a responsibility to desist, change, & act, dissolves denial and enables people to behave coherently with their values—to stop murdering their own kids for the sake of a trip to the mall.

But how do you write about something you can't even think, because it's too big? Bigger than a mind already big enough to contain the universe, but not to contain its pointless, unnecessary ending. Writing comes out as artificial and forced because this has never happened before and there's no colloquial way to say it. The closest you can think of is the Soviet or Nazi terrors. Or the trenches.

You will recall the trenches—mobile graves, fanged with guns. And the elderly, the pompous, & even many of the young women, their future mates, hustling, with their white feathers of cowardice and ostracism, those child-men not just to doom, but to complicit doom where, with strong fingers slippery with blood, they must murder just to earn their own agonising deaths.

What was that if not a mass burnt-offering, of child flesh and child spirit, of child shrieks and child years—so succulent that even a goddess and an angel piled in for a bite, in the persons of Emmeline and Christabel Pankhurst. It's telling that, in their white feather ardour, they never thought to award white feathers to themselves. I mention this only to show how yummy the taste of scorched child meat even to the most shining and admirable; and how smug and blind the sacrificers—nearly as smug and blind as us.

So could this, now, then—also be a child-sacrifice? The escape from the tedium of the goody-goody, into the naughty flames of evil, like a disobedient person who pulls the wings off angels and burns down the world by way of saying 'Won't!' Not negligent at all, but deliberate? A sacrifice extending—on grounds of equity, presumably—this time to female children too? And still the elderly and the vigorous and the gods and the angels, no longer in the persons of suffragettes and retired admirals, but of sporties and luvvies, of journos and politicos and CEOs, hustling the children to their doom just like those bored guards and straining dogs who, with flames for eyes, lined the station platforms of death camps.

And, too, still ensuring it a complicit doom. Before it poisons their skies the children are forced to drink petrol themselves—everything is laced with it—the food, the shelter, the clothes, the parents—there is no way to be clean, even should you wash yourself in it before asking some pretty for a light.

And we dreamed we had left the times of formal sacrifice behind!

Chassez le naturel, il revient au galop, says someone—de Maistre? Chamfort?

But know what? Just as with Rumpelstiltskin, that modest and unambiguous child-molester, by naming it we may go on to stop it, and we shall. We just need the secret spell.

Is it just the two words 'I refuse?' I refuse the disgusting offer to cook my children. I refuse.

Roc Sandford, Gometra, August 2020.

May 2019 Emails: Super-Highway to Rebellion

'For everything to stay the same, everything has to change,' says a character in Giuseppe di Lampedusa's 1963 novel, *The Leopard*. What do we need to change to keep our world stable? How do we solve for X+Y+Z — X being our civilisation's need for energy, without which it will fall swiftly into anarchy; Y being the finite nature of the earth's atmosphere, incapable of absorbing infinite amounts of CO_2 without destroying us; and Z being our understandable wish to live full and happy lives on a healthy planet, followed by future human generations doing the same. *Margaret Atwood*

On Thursday, 23 May 2019, at 14:55, susanamedina@xr.earth wrote:

Roc, great to see you yesterday at the launch of *We'll Never Have Paris*. Thank you for coming! Glad you enjoyed my 'Petite Vilaine'.

Been thinking about your suggestion to do a dialogue … Time is malleable. We could do it both by email and recordings … Here is my first question to you:

You were there at the beginning of Extinction Rebellion. Can you tell me about it? How did you first get involved with XR? And how was it different from previous activism?

If you fancy going out this evening, I'm going to this book-launch about radical environmental movements in the American West, *Surrender* … My friend, Joanna Pocock, has been awarded the Fitzcarraldo Essay prize! The venue looks promising … Leicester Sq … Invite below. Otherwise, we'll meet up soon and do bits of dialogue. Susana x

On Thursday, 23 May 2019, at 17:59, rocsandford@xr.earth wrote:

Hey Susana, great questions—good plan about method. I'm happy to transcribe. And I'll send my answer to your first question tomorrow.

I am in the West End but may be tied up with a mathematical function at the British Academy—will text you if I become free in case you are still around. Otherwise let's conduct dialogue over next few days if that suits. Will you please send me the piece you read at the Rebellion? Rocx

On Friday, 24 May 2019, at 21:55, susanamedina@xr.earth wrote:

Here's the piece I read—

Dear Angelus Novus

Dear Angelus Novus,

Thank you for looking out for me. It was a pleasure to gaze at you while you were at the lake of the critical condition with its bubbles, ripples, currents and patches of green floating bacteria, studying a drifting bottle on its surface, while musing about the existence of extraordinary persons, warts and all, who know why they are here.

You already knew they were here, you had spotted these humans before, protecting all forms of life on the planet, there are many, so many, but at that moment they came to the absolute foreground, like an extreme close-up of laborious ants building ideal cities, which once visited, remain unforgettable, making you know that every single act matters, that you matter, we matter.

You closed your eyes, and tuned into the warm impermanence of things organic. You were suddenly snatched away and propelled elsewhere. In this elsewhere, you felt as if you were orbiting around me in a space capsule and you distinctly heard my strange and eerie wail. You were bewildered to see millions of fragments from dumped satellites and rockets, orbiting around me, promising collisions with new ones, spelling out trouble ahead. Amongst the space junk, you recognised orbiting past a flying aeroplane door, an astronaut's glove, an ejection seat.

Puzzled, you lowered your head, and you were instantly stirred by how intensely blue I am.

You zoomed in, and found me breathtaking.

You were transfixed.

But when you zoomed in further, you were sickened to see plastic rivers, vast islands made of plastic poisoning ocean life, shrinking and vanishing glaciers, asymmetrical segments of broken ice melting adrift on the Artic sea, oil spills, and dead coral reefs. You saw my scars, and you saw vast flooded areas and post-apocalyptic ghost towns with their buildings in ruins. You saw cities of despair and wildfires and drones and abstract patterned lines that happen to be trenches. As you got closer to my surface, you heard the screaming from all this suffering and chaos. You saw shoals of corpses. And you saw starving, homeless and displaced humans from all countries, and the bodies of all the extinct and endangered species.

You then heard thousands of wise children now screaming, now chanting, marching like laborious ants to claim their stolen future, and there were thousands of wise people of all ages, and you wanted to be one of those children, and those yet to be born were also there.

You wept at all this beauty and horror.

You blinked, and I span day into night.

And you loved the night with its silence, and saw my shores brimming with bioluminescent phytoplankton that looked like a stunning starry night, and remembered the beauty of documentaries about luminous life forms on TV, and all the strange and wondrous fauna, flora, insects and minerals you have come across in your life. And you've always been in awe of the sheer diversity of it all. And you wanted to protect me. And you wanted to make better, to repair, to heal, to re-enchant the world. And you wanted to become a luminous life form. And when you landed back on me, you opened your eyes, and you knew why you are here, and once you knew, there was no unknowing.

Thank you once again.

Yours truly,

Planet Earth

On Friday, 24 May 2019, at 22:38, rocsandford@xr.earth wrote:

Querida Susana, thank you for your piece. I love it! Here is my answer. If you think it too long tell me, I can easily cut. And my first question to you is at the end. Rocx

HOW I WAS SUCKED IN

My first memory as a protestor was being pushed by Arnold Wesker in my pushchair into Trafalgar Square on a 60s Ban the Bomb march. I remember the fountains awash with jumping people, the grubby pigeons, the legs of countless marchers wearing drab post-war trousers and pleated skirts. I *think* Bertrand Russell was there. Russell had been brought up by his grandfather in a house in Richmond Park which is now a café—and this grandfather had visited Napoleon on Elba when Napoleon was Emperor of the Elbans. So, it was all a long time ago. And

I remember my dad not coming back from the march. They said he'd been arrested—a new word. Arrest, I was told, was the police locking you in and not letting you out until you knew how to behave. So, I sat on the windowsill looking down into our cobbled street willing him to learn how to behave.

And my second memory of early protest was stopping eating meat and fish, when I was seven. In those days that was subversive, and people couldn't compute who on earth you thought you were, especially since meat rationing had only just ended.

As for XR, I came to it in this way. For a long time, I'd been striving against the Scottish salmon factory farms which, by infecting them with diseases and parasites and maladapted genes, are hustling wild salmon and sea trout populations to extinction. I was getting ever less effective, as the Scottish regulators and environment ministers, captured by salmon industry lobbyists, learned how to exult in cruelty and absorb opposition without reforming.

So, I decided to take a step back, and look at empirical evidence of what kinds of campaigning had brought change. And I was looking at civil disobedience, as Thoreau, albeit posthumously, called it, and trying to figure out how to help start a civil disobedience movement for scientists, when eventually I came to the work of someone called Roger Hallam. This was about January 2018. He'd been studying Martin Luther King, and I suddenly sort of got excited because I saw he was also taking an evidence-based approach to creating change. Because most of us just march or sign petitions or whatever without asking, 'Is this actually going to change anything?' And here was someone who was really thinking hard about it and seeing what had worked.

So, I was stirred by that. This was about five in the morning because I couldn't sleep, and I saw on Twitter that Roger was saying: 'Please come to Marble Arch by 7 a.m. if you are willing to sit down in front of the traffic.' I'd often dreamed of sitting down in front of the traffic, but I've never wanted to alone, and I'd never found anyone else before who wanted to. I happened to be in London so, like someone fast-forwarding a grainy movie, I instantly got out of bed and got on my bicycle (having dressed) and cycled through the night to Marble Arch. There I sat down with about fifteen other people in front of the rush-hour traffic.

Drivers then were less familiar with 'swarming' (blocking the traffic) and some of the commuters were livid. They'd rather we didn't inconvenience them while they were poisoning our air and helping slaughter our children. It was scary because a few of them would use their cars to suddenly lurch forwards as if to kill us, but then stop just in time. And they would climb out of their cars with reddened faces, and shout. Or, more comically, strut about wearing tight jeans and cowboy boots and videoing us.

I found it difficult. Few of us like thwarting people. We don't like stopping people doing what they want to do. So, if you're doing that, it's actually unpleasant, you feel really bad. I had to overcome that feeling and realise that I had to do this, even if it meant I was being rude in thwarting the business-as-usual of mass-slaughter and extinction.

One of the commuters, as I was sitting crossed-legged on the road in front of the revving cars, kicked me between the eyes. I went over backwards and hit my head on the tarmac, and started slurring my words. For a few months, I lost my sense of smell, and could no longer whistle. And I lost the feeling in one of my legs. But I remember thinking—that's it, I've actually smashed my face against the terrifying machine which is busy grinding us all up. Stopping this machine can't be costless, especially if you use your face, and I accepted the damage as the price of being allowed to help affront the evil. I went to St Mary's hospital, but they didn't have any doctors available, so they gave me a photocopy of a leaflet about head injuries. Roger later dubbed me 'the first casualty of the Rebellion' which I like to contract to 'first casualty', as in 'first lady'. Anyhow, those protests later evolved into XR, with its signature use of non-violent direct action or NVDA.

Now, tell me what paths led you to XR, because I think when we first met, you too were already rebelling.

Rocx

On Friday, 24 May 2019, at 23:55, susanamedina@xr.earth wrote:

Roc, how beautiful the beginning of your answer ...

I'm so shocked by what you're telling me! This guy who kicked you hard in the face wasn't arrested? He got into his car and drove away?

It's terrible. I'm so sorry. Can't get my head round it. A big hug from here.

So, you had concussion? I can't detect any slurring ... The trauma of being attacked, though, must have lasted for several months ...

A big big hug,

I'll (try to) answer your question tomorrow.

Sx

On Saturday, 25 May 2019, at 14:24, susanamedina@xr.earth wrote:

Roc,

Here, my answer. Sx

WHAT DREW ME IN

The reality of climate change has been staring at us for a long time now. It's a tragedy. Inaction is a tragedy. And it's indeed criminal. I've been reading about climate change, pollution and environmental triggers to illness for quite a few years. It's a general interest, and it's part of my research for my novel *Spinning Days of Night*. In 1998, I was really ill, and when I got a bit better, though still frail, I started going for walks. Something very strange happened, a kind of ecophany. I felt in my very bones that if I went to Kilburn High Street I would die. Kilburn High Street is a solid block of pollution and I felt my body wouldn't be able to withstand the damage. It's where I do my shopping and I avoided going there for two months. I wrote about it. At the time, I didn't know that air pollution causes 64,000 early deaths in the UK every year. Worldwide, it's 8.8 million early deaths a year! This figure is from a new study published this March in the *European Heart Journal*, previous estimates were wrong, much lower. The study concludes we need to switch to clean energy urgently.

Last year, googling about environmental triggers to illness, I came across the two-week hunger strike in protest at the new Heathrow runway. That was in September 2018. I was aware of the expansion's disastrous long-term impact on both air pollution and climate change, as it would make Heathrow the single biggest carbon emitter in the UK. I watched a video with Robin Boardman speaking about the need for mass civil disobedience to reduce carbon dioxide pollution to zero by 2025. I was interested in the fact that a new generation was leading the hunger strike. The articles I read mentioned XR.

So, XR was suddenly on my Twitter feed. I didn't know much about the sixth mass extinction. To begin with, some of the wording sounded cult-like and apocalyptic, and I soon became alarmed at the catastrophic levels of ecological collapse as I started to follow other related accounts, like *Arctic News*. Let's say, the full horror ... seized me with its fangs. Also, I could see Gandhi at the core of XR's philosophy. To me, Gandhi is gold. He's one of the politicians I respect the most, and that, of course, includes his ecological vision. A good friend, Lorna Scott Fox, became an XR Legal Observer and also organised a Rebel Riders Swarm where we had to dress as bees. We also blocked four highly polluted crossings in Bethnal Green Road, Tower Hamlets. I started leafletting and speaking to passers-by about the need to declare a Climate Emergency. A festival with music, speeches and free food had been organised in a small green area. There were so many families, activities for children, including XR Symbol body transfers, and the atmosphere was green electric. I continued leafletting in the tube, and from then onwards, wherever I went. But I didn't go to any XR workshops, nor did I want any responsibilities. I was snowed under with work and caring for my mother, and was also determined not to get distracted by anything, as I wanted to finish my novel, but moving paragraphs around became increasingly pointless. I was seeing all these XR events in social media and not going, but retweeting, reading about them avidly, and feeling a pressure to act in the real world. I went to the first Climate Youth Strike in London and was immensely moved by the audacity of children and teenagers. It became increasingly obvious that joining the Rebellion on the 15th of April 2019 for its whole duration, whatever that was, was much more important than tinkering with my novel. I had to make time. In any case, it was all interrelated. The Rebellion surpassed my wildest dreams. Though of course, the struggle isn't over.

Now here are my next questions—

There are so many eco-struggles to choose from. Was there anything you witnessed directly that made you realise that Scottish salmon factory farms were driving salmon and sea trout to extinction?

There were many things that fascinated me about XR as I got to know the movement better. What kind of things fascinated you about XR?

Sx

On Monday, 27 May 2019, at 23:31, rocsandford@xr.earth wrote:

Dear Susana—Thank you, your answer is lovely too!

Here are my answers to your questions. If my answers are too long we can easily cut them down later. Let's accumulate material and then edit it down. Rocx

WHAT WAS DONE TO THE SALMON

Thirty years ago I went to live on Gometra, a deserted island hidden somewhere off the Atlantic coast of Scotland. It's off grid, and you feel you are living both how everyone used to, and how everyone will. That's why I like reading the Soviet era poets—at least those who straddled the bourgeois and Soviet times—Akhmatova, Tsvetaeva, Mandelstam. It is interesting they had no opposite numbers I can think of in the Nazi terror, except perhaps the prose writers—Kertész, Wiesel, Frank. Soviet poetry, Nazi prose! These books seem not to be so much about their present, as our future, given what is coming and can be lessened, but no longer averted.

Anyhow, on Gometra, the wild salmon, enormous gleaming fish, used to scull in from the Atlantic and follow the cliffs on both sides of the island on their way to the lovely River Ba, where they would mate and spawn. When I first went to live there the numbers of wild salmon were already dropping, as vast plumes of parasites coming from the recently installed salmon farms off the nearby Isle of Ulva ate the passing wild salmon alive—even their eyes. It's sometimes called the 'crown of bones', when the parasites, which are called sea-lice, eat all the way through to a living wild salmon's skull. Likewise, the sea trout used to jump out of the water where the burns run into the sea, but you never see them now. The RSPCA—to its immortal shame—licences and condones these farms—even the Soil Association, which should know better, has been implicated in some of them.

So that set me looking at the research. I was so shocked by many things—too many to go through here. But to give just one example, it turns out there are fat-soluble carcinogens and birth-defect chemicals in Scottish farmed salmon which stay in your body for the rest of your life. Jérôme Ruzzin, one of the researchers in this area, has pointed out that if you have already eaten Scottish farmed salmon, there still is a way to get the carcinogens out of your body, which is to have a baby. The carcinogens leave your body via the placenta and in the breast-milk.

But it's not just wild salmon and babies that are being harmed. The Scottish salmon companies shoot seals, and poison crustaceans, and use underwater alarms which illegally disturb dolphins, whales and porpoises, and the Scottish Government, which must also be somehow in on the racket, turns a blind eye. In trashing the biodiversity on which our lives depend, these ill-informed cynics have betrayed the trust we place in them, and must be replaced. But when I started trying to warn people, all this was not much known about, and I was physically cornered and threatened with violence, shamed in the press, and ostracised and trolled by salmon farm fans. Living alone, as I did, I slept with an axe under my bed for self-defence—the kind of axe you see in fairy-tales. Two different people said my house would be burned down. And then by-standers always pile into a shaming—smelling blood, they get creamy—it's the phenomenon of the crowd, that Sphinx whose riddle, says Le Bon, you must crack lest it devour you. Some of the Salmon farm fans tried to figure out things I had done wrong myself, and denounced me to the authorities. The embarrassingly high-ranking official sent from the mainland to investigate (I think of the police sergeant in *The Wicker Man*) was kind enough to laugh at the absurdity. So, I was lucky. Everyone knows more about it now, but the Scottish government is still planning to double the size of the salmon industry within a few years. They must be stopped before, in their serial-killer frenzy, they massacre the sea.

And WHAT WAS NEW ABOUT XR

To answer your second question, what fascinated me about XR at first was that there were other people willing to do what I wanted to do—sit down in front of the traffic. I had always remembered that nameless person with his shopping bag who stood in front of the tanks at Tiananmen Square. Nobody knows what happened to him. Is he alive? Nobody even knows what happened to his family, or to the tank drivers, or their families. But I knew we all needed to do what he did, if only we were as brave as him—and not just with tanks, but cars and planes.

And then, I liked XR's use of evidence—see what has worked in the past—Gandhi, MLK, the Suffragettes—and emulate it. I was trained as a natural scientist, so the empiricism in this appealed to me. I didn't know it would work, but I believed it had the best chance of anything I had seen.

And then I was drawn by the iconography of XR—the typeface, the colours, the flags, the symbols, the beauty and precision of the design. So powerful—like the unforgettable iconography of early Soviet times. It invited you in—it dissolved exclusion—it's as if, due to the iconography, you were already inside, and had been all along.

And I liked the training—how to give the XR talk, to be a spokesperson, to facilitate a meeting, to be arrested, to go to prison, or go on hunger-strike. And of course, I liked the free food, the money-free environments, and—above all, the people!

And the autonomy. I loved that. Anti-bureaucrats. If you respected the ten principles, and were advancing the three demands, whatever you did *was* XR.

Now tell me what fascinated you. And tell me, too, what happened to you during the Easter Rebellion? You helped me build my portable pond on Waterloo Bridge, and visited me when I was locked-on under the lorry to stop the police being able to drag it away. And we were at Piccadilly Circus together when it was occupied by XR Youth too. What a blissful dawn that was!

On Tuesday, 28 May 2019, at 23:13, susanamedina@xr.earth wrote:

Yes, it was magical! And what a coincidence we met with both our families right on the first morning of the Rebellion, at Piccadilly Circus, where I was reading 'Dear Angelus Novus', when I kjmmmmmmmmmmmmmmmmmm+ (Ooops, my cat Magic's intervention!) barely knew you, and had just messaged you to meet on Waterloo Bridge in the evening. Initially, I was going to be part of the Rebellion on Marble Arch, as I had a friend there. But doing a garden on Waterloo Bridge proved irresistible, and it was direct on my tube line. So, was so pleased we walked there together, as I didn't know anyone. I instantly adopted you as my affinity group. My mum and brother joined us there, to see my reading for Letters to the Earth on the stage-truck, hosted by Leslie Stuart Tate. It was a bit scary, as the police were really hustling us to leave, but we stayed put and managed to do the readings. It was so nerve-racking!

But, to return to your question …

WHAT FASCINATED ME?

Following XR on Twitter I got a sense of an unfolding intelligence. And I could see imagination was key. And that fascinated me. There was a sense of urgency, and it was non-hierarchical. The XR actions that I was seeing were very much related to collective performance art, and aesthetically, it was interesting as well. And all this reinforced my willingness to support XR. The fact that they were producing this media dialogue through images that were beautiful, shocking and humorous. Like when I saw the Garden Bridge (Waterloo Bridge) as one of the International Rebellion sites, I thought that was very humorous, a great up-yours to Boris Johnson's astronomically expensive, failed Garden Bridge project. And I just I loved the idea, and wanted to be part of it.

PS: But look, let's meet and talk—it might be more interesting than writing emails. What are you doing tomorrow night?

May 2019 Dialogue: Paolozzi Rendezvous

Paolozzi Rendezvous

Perhaps it was this absence of personal memories that made Kerans indifferent to the spectacle of these sinking civilisations. He had been born and brought up entirely within what had once been known as the Arctic Circle—now a sub-tropical zone with an annual mean temperature of eighty-five degrees—and had come southward only on joining one of the ecological surveys in his early 30's. The vast swamps and jungles had been a fabulous laboratory, the submerged cities little more than elaborate pedestals.

Apart from a few older men such as Bodkin there was no-one who remembered living in them—and even during Bodkin's childhood the cities had been beleaguered citadels, hemmed in by enormous dykes and disintegrated by panic and despair, reluctant Venices to their marriage with the sea. Their charm and beauty lay precisely in their emptiness, in the strange junction of two extremes of nature, like a discarded crown overgrown by wild orchids. *J. G. Ballard*

Rebel Palace, 31st May, 2019. Scene: The concert hall of the flooded and collapsing former Paddington Conservative Club, now the site of the tent in which Roc camps when in London.

'Would you like some cider, Susana?' 'Yes, please! ... Roc, can you do all the talking? I've been editing all day and I'm a bit ...' 'Unfocused?' 'Yep.' 'Okay.'

Art of Digression

Roc: So, Susana.

Susana: Are you going to ask me a question? That's cheating!

Roc: Well, that's normal for interviews.

Susana: All right. Okay. No, I thought you speak first as in you say—whatever. Okay. You can ask me a question.

Roc: So, when I saw you, I think at the *Finneganight,* you were wearing a skirt with a symbol embroidered on it. Can you tell me about that symbol?

Susana: Well, it's the XR symbol. It's a stylised hourglass, time running out, inside a circle, which represents the planet ... Borges often mentions the hourglass in his writing ... And that colourful skirt has two big circles, and I just took it to Waterloo Bridge and had the XR symbol block-printed on it. I like the idea of becoming the message. XR's Arts Factory is great with all these stalls with block-printing of XR symbols. Most people who come across them want to become the message! But the hourglass is—I love it as an object. It's the perfect symbol!

Roc: The hourglass also looks a little like the pictures of women they put on ladies' toilets. They have someone wearing a skirt which is like the bottom bit of the hourglass, and the torso is the top.

Susana: You know what it also looks like? Like Midland Bank's symbol, but vertical.

Roc: Interesting. Yeah. And I've noticed if you turn it on the side, it looks like Spiderman's face.

Susana: I read an interview with ESP, the guy who designed the XR symbol, and it seems like he approached different ecological NGOs to see whether they would be interested, and they said, 'No.' They said, 'It wasn't an interesting symbol,' which amazes me because I just think it really works.

Roc: It's powerful.

Susana: And he and artist Carrie Reichardt made a mosaic with the symbol to begin with.

Roc: I wonder where that is. It perhaps is with the pink boat and the bridge lorry.

Susana: It exists. It's a tangible thing.

Roc: It might be where the great icons of XR are. The pink boat. And the lorry.

Susana: Where's the boat?

Roc: And where is the lorry?

Susana: Where's the boat?

Roc: I don't know. But I don't know where the mosaic is either. And maybe they're all in the same place XR never-never-land?

Susana: XR Heaven! I might be wrong because I'm thinking of Paolozzi and mosaics in the tube, but when I saw it, it reminded me of him, because of geometry, abstraction and the fact that it's a mosaic. So, I associate the XR symbol mosaic with the tube. I think it's somewhere in east London ... Tower Hamlets, maybe.

Roc: I have a Paolozzi that he made for me.

Susana: You what?

Roc: Which is the dog over there.

Susana: What, Paolozzi made that dog for you?

Roc: Yeah.

Susana: Amazing. I'll look at it later. That's amazing. He made it for you because?

Roc: Actually, he made that one for my son Cato, and the one he made for me is in the other room. It says 'Roc' on it.

Susana: (Looking at Paolozzi dog.) Okay. That's very un-Paolozzi.

Roc: That's partly why I like it. It's so funny, to have a non-Paolozzi Paolozzi. My gran was a collector of his very early and a friend of his. So I knew him all my life.

Susana: All right. Okay. Do you have any other Paolozzis that you got from your grandmother?

Roc: I have one or two prints and things, but there are more in my family. One which is very, very beautiful, which is a table with all sorts of strange things sticking out of it. So, as a table it's useless because there's no room to put anything down. It's made of bronze, but it's incredibly beautiful. More table than a table.

Susana: Well, that's interesting. I don't know Paolozzi's work that well, but he's worked on spirals. He was close friends with J. G. Ballard.

Roc: Was he? I didn't know that. I love Ballard. Only, he doesn't understand how good a writer he is, and therefore isn't.

Susana: His writing is fascinating, and prescient. There's this quote of his I've used a couple of times when writing about the brain as an erogenous organ: 'One looks forward to the day when the General Theory of Relativity and the Principia will outsell the Kama Sutra in back-street bookshops.' Good, yeah? ... Back to Paolozzi, you know I told you sometimes I ask my dreams questions? There was this time I asked my dream a question, and J. G. Ballard turned up and directed me to Paolozzi's work on spirals. So, I wrote about spirals.

Roc: Interesting. I haven't seen that, but I love spirals too ... Shall I show you my spiral flag made by my daughter Blue?

Susana: Could do.

Roc: It's just here.

Susana: It's great. It's very good. Spirals are fascinating.

Roc: They are fascinating, and this flag is about nature disappearing down a whirlpool and the whale is disappearing in the middle.

Susana: The Climate Death Spiral flag! We were talking before about putting the XR flag on the mast at the front of your house. Maybe you should put this one too! ... So, the Paolozzi dog, that was a nice present! It's not very XR, but it's very interesting ... Your grandmother collecting.

Roc: Yes, my grandmother collected art. She didn't have any money, but she had some nice paintings, and she had friends who were artists. Kokoschka was a friend of hers and painted a picture of her. He gave her the most beautiful bright brown eyes, while in life her eyes were bright blue. She complained about that, which perhaps contained an unbecoming aesthetic judgement.

Susana: So, she had good friends. That was her way of becoming a collector?

Roc: Exactly. If you like owning art, you either have to be rich or have friends who are artists.

Susana: Or have a lot of charm.

Roc: Or have a lot of charm, yeah. There is one other way which a friend told me which is terrible. I mean it's a terrible story, but I will tell it to you. Which is there is an abortion doctor in Harley Street who allegedly has paintings, lots of Freuds, lots of paintings by heterosexual artists, but no Bacons, none by homosexual artists. And the artist would pay with a painting for an abortion.

Susana: So, I should think they weren't necessarily female artists because men could also pay for it?

Roc: I haven't seen his collection, and I expect he's died by now. It was someone from the fifties and sixties. It's like the picture of Dorian Grey but the other way round; the portraits the portraits of people who had never been.

Susana: Well, you know, it's a form of payment. You get dentists, I know one dentist in Cologne that you can get dental treatment—

Roc: And restaurants. There was a restaurant called *Meridiana* near South Kensington and Paolozzi did a sculpture that went on the outside of it, so you could see it looking down the street from the tube station. And in return he got free meals there, I think as much as he wanted for the rest of his life. He took me there when I was a child and told me the story. It made me decide to be an artist because it was an escape from money and besides, the pasta was seductive.

Susana: I wish you could do that with writing for many things.

Roc: You can do it with writing ... but it has to be on a cheque.

Susana: With rare exceptions, nobody gives us anything, apart from cheap wine.

Roc: Well, I think writing is interesting because you can make as many copies as you want of it, and that is so powerful because it means almost everyone can have a copy. If they can read, and have time to, which is a big if. And painting, not everyone can have it.

Susana: Well, if it's in a public collection.

Roc: People can see it, but when they're shown in public collections, it's cold. It's like being in an airport. It's not good for the paintings. And I have a suspicion that the paintings are put there to subtract their disruptive power.

Susana: If you see paintings in a palace or in a church or in an important private collection, it's not like an airport, but it also has ideological connotations, just as the idea of the white cube has. With modern art, with what is considered 'great art,' many times it's about the space where it's shown. The space is so monumental. So, you're completely awed by the space. You go to the Royal Academy, wherever you go, the space is already amazing, and it calls for monumentality, for a certain size to the works. Now, not many artists can work on that kind of size because you must be able to afford that kind of studio, and some artists might not want that kind of monumentality.

Roc: I went to *Frieze Masters* maybe two or three years ago, which is *Frieze* but for old paintings and sculptures and things, and there was a beautiful installation there which was someone's very messy fifties flat with some beautiful art in it. And the art looked so much better in this messy flat than it does in galleries. I was really moved. And when I looked at the label, I was so surprised and pleased, because the installation turned out to be by N., a friend of mine. I hadn't seen him for a while, so I asked him round, and when he got to my house he kind of melted—because it's very messy here too, with lots of interesting art, just like his installation.

Susana: When I was curating projects in abandoned spaces, which was what got us talking when we first met, it was about creating a different type of environment, rather than housing art in a white cube. And it was about showing art in the street as well. We did art on billboards and that kind of thing.

Roc: Very good. Yeah! I think that's more interesting. I mean I suppose the thing about big public galleries, you do see the art that's good enough to overcome the setting. It's clear to you if it's strong enough to overcome. But then a lot of the art isn't good enough to overcome the setting but is still in there.

Tragedy, Humour, Clarity

Susana: So, anyway, for a while, the XR symbol artist wasn't very lucky with getting green organisations to use it. I'm referring to the circled hourglass.

Roc: But it's not just that symbol. XR has other symbols that are also beautiful, like the bees. Or the skull of a goat.

Susana: Or the butterfly with *Rebel* for Life or Rebel *for Life*. That's one of the things that I like: the slogans, the simplicity of the demands. You know: 'Act now.' 'Tell the Truth.' 'Rebel for Life', if you are generally a rebel, is going to draw you in. And then, there is the command: 'Rebel for Life', because we must act to protect life.

Roc: I like the double meaning, and the iconography and the art and the very simple slogans or mottoes are beautiful.

Susana: The XR designers who come up with the slogans have been really clever, and it's all about clarity. What I also enjoyed was that there were collective performances all the time. This idea of performance and theatricality and that it was there to give an image to the media as well. So, actions like the pouring out of red paint in 'Blood of Our Children', I was so pleased to see it circulating so much in the media. The performance Culture Declares Emergency did at Tate Modern, with the white horse and the grass coats and the singing. And the speaking to Tate Modern in its own language. It's fascinating to see XR engaging with different institutions in their own language. Of course, when these rebels went to Parliament and got semi-naked and glued themselves, I just thought that was fantastic.

So, XR does have a lot of humour as well and cheekiness in the way it deals with protest. I enjoy that. The fact that there were gigs and plays at Waterloo Bridge's stage truck. There was a very interesting play about fossil fuels. And generally, rebels also willing to dress the part for whatever XR is doing. Like now let's dress in black or let's dress as bees or let's dress in red—the aspect of collective performance. Like when rebels parodied Fashion Week in Oxford Circus. It was gorgeous and hilarious. Cultural references are always there. And there's this situationist element ...

Roc: It's a little like rediscovering childhood.

Susana: It's play.

Roc: That one is allowed again to play.

Susana: The spirit of carnival. The carnivalesque.

Naked Rebels in Parliament

Roc: I like the way you said that each institution is addressed in its own language like the Tate is addressed in grass and Parliament in nakedness, and Downing Street in blood. There is a terrible truth there.

My daughter Blue was one of the people who poured the blood outside Downing Street. My son Lazer did his A-level maths revision with his neck D-locked to the Palace of Westminster. And my daughter Savannah, you mentioned the House of Commons naked action, her job was to go into the visitors' gallery in the House of Commons and take off her clothes and get in the way of the security guards.

Susana: Oh, really?

Roc: So that the guards in the gallery would be blocked by her and not be able to get to everyone else who were also taking off their clothes and gluing-on to the big window above the MPs.

Susana: That's great! So, Savannah did that? That's fantastic!

Roc: So, Savannah did that, but I'll tell you what happened next. She took off her clothes. The guards all saw her. But the other people according to the plan were taking off their clothes and gluing themselves to the glass. And the guards saw that too, but Savannah was in their way. So, they pushed Savannah out through the door of the gallery into the midst of a group of astonished tourists waiting to come into the visitors' gallery, slammed the door behind her, and went to deal with the glue-ons. Then she realised she had nobody holding her, and just went back in. She could have glued-on herself, but like me she has a thing about glue. Then they pushed her out again, and she asked if she could take her clothes. They said 'Of course not!' and slammed the door again. And Savannah was then in the position where she was naked except for her knickers, and she realised that if she could only slip out of the House of Commons, she wouldn't be in trouble. All she had to do is leave the House of Commons while naked. But that was a bit of a funny task. Like in a dream, when you suddenly have no clothes, at a party, with the Emperor.

Susana: So what did she do then?

Roc: She borrowed a jacket off someone, and she borrowed a jumper off someone which she wrapped around her waist, and when she got to the bottom of the spiral staircase, at the octagonal gallery which leads to the chambers for the members and peers, she started running, barefoot, which gave the game away a bit, and she says she heard more and more shouts of 'Stop Police' getting gruffer and gruffer. And in the end, she decided she'd better stop. After all, they have guns. Automatics. And so she was caught by lots of police people in this very beautiful Gothic revival gallery lined with statues and murals which I'm sure she will remember forever.

Susana: Was she arrested?

Roc: And she was arrested. Yeah. She was charged with 'Outraging Public Decency.'

Susana: She's so beautiful. How can she possibly outrage anyone?

Roc: She might have to go to court.

Susana: Oh, that'd be an enviable criminal record So, a distraction was created. Many times, with certain events, I wonder about the logistics of some XR actions. How did that happen?

Roc: So well planned!

Susana: I love it. I just loved it!

Roc: Me too. I thought it was brilliant. And I loved the expression of one of the MPs. His eyes popped.

Susana: Yes, Milliband.

What Children Know

Roc: Nietzsche says that morality reduces to aesthetics. Moral decisions are really aesthetic decisions and XR, in making the movement very aesthetic, kind of reinforces the morality. If you make it beautiful you can convey that it's good in some way.

Susana: Yes. Because you already agree with the aesthetics. Though of course, it's open to manipulation. The Nazis used aesthetics to lure their citizens. But with XR, I think of *The Society of the Spectacle*. XR uses media-friendly spectacular images, which is the language our society uses to sell us lifestyles, so as to wake people into a different awareness, the reality of our predicament. It constructs photogenic radical situations which reorder our consciousness. So, I could see Debord's *détournement* in action: the use of spectacular images and language to disrupt the flow of the spectacle. That really interested me ... But going back to your children, it's so wonderful that all of them are part of XR. Could you tell me how they got into it, and how they started coming up with actions and so forth?

Roc: Well, I was very involved with it. They must have seen me doing it and thought: what was I doing? And next thing I knew, they were all outclassing me, easily.

And my oldest child, Cato, isn't, because he's in India putting solar panels into villages. So, I can't remember exactly how they got drawn into it. I had lots of XR people living here in the house early on. So, it could be that was how they got turned as it were.

Susana: That's good. You must be so proud of your children.

Roc: Extremely proud, yeah. And I also feel pleased because I think they're just learning incredible things. And all their lives they've been in either a family or a school, and they're going into this other world, which is a really real environment, and the most vital thing that anyone could be doing.

Susana: Very special.

Roc: Yeah, special, and demanding. And needing courage and needing ingenuity, love, generosity, compassion, self-control. But at the same time, it's also ... it can be dark, because one is thinking about the future, and one is facing the terrible truths that it's easier not to face. So, it can be dark for them as well and I worry about that.

Susana: They must be truly anxious about the future.

Roc: Yeah, because I think a lot of people are protected from the knowledge, especially children and young people. XR is an environment where you're not protected from the knowledge, and you do have to confront it and face it.

Susana: The Youth Strike ... Fridays for Future are really upfront with the science about our planet. Children and teenagers are really aware of what's happening to it. They're leading the debate on climate change, with all these lovely placards, actions, videos and Twitter accounts.

Roc: They are! And XR Youth! But XR itself has been central to making the media and politicians start to admit the horror of the problem, so everyone can learn and figure out how to change and what to demand of the leaders.

Re: Easter Rebellion, 2019

The words that reverberate for us at the confines of this long adventure of rebellion are not formulas for optimism, for which we have no possible use in the extremities of our unhappiness, but words of courage and intelligence which, on the shores of the eternal seas, even have the qualities of virtue.
Albert Camus

Rebel Rebel

Susana: When I watched *Pond Rebel*, the video diary that you've done about the Easter Rebellion, at the beginning you mention that the Rebellion is about to start, you mention children and you're almost tearful. Were you fearful for your children?

Roc: I was fearful for my children during the Easter Rebellion. But I was way, way more fearful for the future. And so, the real fear is for the future, I mean that's probably what made me want to cry. And the feeling of children actually stopping that future is moving and beautiful but also upsetting. So, I think that's what it was. I was scared. I was more scared then than now. It might be too late now for the authorities to really crack down on XR in Britain, because there might be too many people, and they maybe can't lock up 50,000 people. Might not be too late, we'll see.

So then maybe the Easter Rebellion was the last moment at which the authorities could have really nipped it, by being unexpectedly vicious and I was scared that that would happen. And I think there's also ... Well, like I've said my experience has been a certain amount of harassment and smearing and shaming and various ways that I've been seriously harmed by whatever forces I've stood up against, and I can see that the forces that XR is fighting are so, so powerful and ruthless. So, there is apprehension there, but my real apprehension is about the future.

Susana: Courage and patience are vital. There will be forces trying to harm XR.

Roc: Definitely. And trying to harm the individuals and discredit the individuals and sabotage it all. I think there will be *agents provocateurs* and also entryists from other groups discrediting the movement by being violent or by whatever. And XR has grown so fast that it's possible it could split, because people disagree about what non-violence is, for example. There's lots of difficult things that could happen in the future. What's happened already is beautiful and decisive and people underestimate how effective it's been. But I don't think the future is necessarily easy. There may be problems. It's just that XR looks like our best hope, so we have to overcome the problems as they come.

Susana: But apart from XR, we need everyone to come together, not just under XR, but under the banner of 'Let's save the planet'. And there are so many diverse groups and different ways of bringing that together. So that's what we have to emphasise.

Roc: Absolutely. Let's not kill the planet.

Susana: Because some people might not want to be arrested or might not ... I heard someone I know, say 'Oh they're such a hippy bunch. All those hippies on Waterloo Bridge!' Some people might not want to be associated with a certain look ... But there were people from all walks of life and ages and it was very varied. Some people associate the Rebellion with New Age hippies or students. And they don't want to be part of that. Maybe there could be an XR for executives and city people. That would be good!

Roc: That was why, when the Declaration of Rebellion happened in October 2018, I wore a suit. I wanted people to see that it was different kinds of people who were declaring rebellion.

Susana: Were you in Parliament Square?

Roc: Yes.

Susana: I didn't see you. What a pity!

Roc: You probably thought I was a businessman and didn't notice me. Or an MP. I had a tie and a white shirt and ... Because I think if on the news they see police dragging away someone in a suit and tie, it's a little bit more shocking for the viewers on their sofas.

Susana: Maybe we should all wear suits and ties for the next actions. Or police costumes! But that's true, wearing suits and then being dragged away … that would be an effective image.

I was ecstatic when the Climate Emergency was declared in Parliament. About an hour later, I saw Fox, the lovely XR Media guy, in Trafalgar Square with the Red Brigade, and hugging him, I started screaming 'We won!' while whirling around with him. We were dancing and he was saying, 'We haven't won yet!' Of course, he was right. His camera was recording and it was posted on Facebook. It was a continuation of the Carnival of Chaos, in which we demanded protection for rainforests and justice for Indigenous peoples and earth protectors outside the Brazilian Embassy. A friend sent me the video. It's hilarious. I will send it to you.

Roc: Good, yeah. Have you thought about doing a video diary yourself? Like *Pond Rebel?*

Susana: No. There was something silly that I did, but I really enjoyed it, and I recorded myself a bit. You know these little bits of fabric with 'Rebel for Life', 'Act Now', 'Tell the Truth' and so forth? There was one which read 'Hot for Activists', so I made a headband with it, and wore it, and talked to a lot of people on Waterloo Bridge. Especially when I felt that they weren't rebels. It was my way of recruiting new rebels, and then I thought 'Maybe I'm also freaking out a lot of people?' The sun was blazing, and I was really having fun. And then I went into the Hayward to get some water and there were these guys wearing sleek suits and I said, pointing at the headband: 'Do I look good?' Because they were obviously not activists and looked really anal. And they said 'No.' I don't know who they were, but they were at the Hayward and they were so horrible. I don't know, it was just being really silly. I felt so free!

Roc: I always think that somewhere like the Hayward is doing us a service because all the people like that just go there and it means they're not anywhere else.

Susana: The Hayward was completely empty, except for those two people.

Roc: Ok, ok! Now, I'm always trying to step back and see the deeper problem. Maybe it's bigger than consumerism, but we are put into an artificial state where we're not ourselves. And the artificial state is the consumer state where we need to consume holidays, and cars, and carbonated energy, and things we don't need, which stop us actually living our lives. They are simulated lives, which are substituted for the real lives that were much richer. The Rebellion was real life again and uncommercial. It was interesting to see so many people interacting without money. I didn't see any money. I'm not sure whether I spent any money for the whole duration of the Rebellion, actual coins or anything.

Susana: Yes, there were all these rebel cooks, yum-yum food, it was well organised, and it was about a set of values that are, you know, just wonderful and good for you, good for the planet. Like living in an eco-society, no aggression, of course, non-violence. You could really feel there was absolutely and honestly not a shred of aggression. Instead, there was this refreshing willingness to cooperate and be there, and all the emphasis on love, empathy, compassion, frugality and everyone sharing that message. It was wonderful enacting it as a collective. It was invigorating, and above all, transformative.

Roc: It was wonderful.

Susana: It was very, very special. I did an induction on Waterloo Bridge, and I met some new rebels there who were very much into love, love, love, love, love, especially in the WhatsApp messages we sent each other, with all these green hearts and nice emojis ... We soon found out we also shared Bowie in our DNA, and I sent them the homage I wrote to him. So, that was my affinity group. It was called 'Waterloo Sunset', we called each other 'Sunsets', and it was good.

Do No Harm

Roc: More cider, Susana? Talking of consumerism. Shall I fetch another bottle?

Susana: If you'll share it with me. I've been meaning to ask you ... As a scientist, do you feel that a crime has been committed against the scientific community, because all these things have been known for a long time, and maybe some solutions could have happened by now, such as technologies that would not rely on fossil fuels?

Roc: It's a crime against everyone. Not just the scientists.

Susana: It is against everyone, of course.

Roc: Yeah, and the artificially cheap energy that we have at the moment, I don't think it can be replaced. We can't live in the same way as we live now by finding another way of doing it. I don't think that's realistic. I may be entirely wrong. People might figure out how to use fusion or something. But it's not that we can go on living in the same way without fossil fuels as we did with them. The way we live will be different. I don't think we will be able to fly or drive around like we do now. But I think on the positive side, it will be nicer. Like, I haven't flown for 10 years, maybe more, and it's not a vow, I may even fly again, I don't know, especially if I decide to leave Europe or when we reach the *sauve qui peut* moment. But for 10 or 15 years I haven't been in an aeroplane. I can recommend it. It's a relief. Like giving up head-banging for Lent.

Susana: We once talked about people not taking flights to go home and visit their lovers, their friends, because if all this greenhouse gas pollution continues, there'll be no home, no lovers, no friends ... Like many climate scientists and environmentalists, you stopped driving, flying, and at home, you sacrifice a lot of things to reduce your carbon footprint: you have no central heating, you use solar panels, you don't use hot water. You've made a series of very radical decisions, haven't you?

Roc: Yeah. I'm in no way perfect and I've got miles to go, but I felt ... I could see it was harming the small cosmic bubble of life I lived on. Like the little prince's planet, and hardly bigger. It wasn't going to make much difference, me not flying, but I didn't want to take part. I wanted to begin to withdraw, even if I couldn't stop it, and even if I couldn't withdraw completely from my own part in the harm, I just wanted to make it ever less if I could.

It's like when terrible, bad things are being done. You can't withdraw completely because your whole environment is tainted. But you can begin to withdraw. So I got rid of the car. But I've still got miles to go, we all have. The harm is hidden everywhere in our culture, and you can't not be complicit—that's how it works, to make us all complicit, and then make out any resistance is hypocrisy.

The reason I raised this is because it's a relief not to fly, because you're programmed to think you want to fly, but actually if you forgo it, you may be happier. Partly because there's subliminal guilt from flying and you know you shouldn't. And partly because it's really unpleasant the way you're treated up there and while waiting to get on. And partly because you need lots of money to pay for the tickets and may have to do unpleasant things or forgo doing nice things to get it. And partly because your soul can't travel by plane anyway and gets left behind and has to trudge overland, and by the time it catches up you're back in the airport with your baggage waiting for the strike to be over so you can go home.

Susana: My soul can certainly travel by plane while looking at the cloud ceiling, the amazing cloudscape you can see from the window! And, well, there's the pleasure of destination ... For people who have travelled a lot and seen lots of places, to stop flying might not be such a sacrifice ... but for the young not to be able to explore the world, it's such a pity. The problem is how planes are powered and their deadly pollution—we should certainly try to ban private jets ... The sky is filled with bad omens. But travelling is wonderful. Seeing different places is wonderful. Of course, you can see them on the internet. It's not same as being physically in India or wherever.

Roc: Yes, but you can go to India in a train. And trains use fossil fuels, but much less than planes. And the reason people can't is because they have a job, partly so that they can pay for their flights. A lot of what we're doing is having jobs so we can buy a car, we can go away on holiday, we can spend lots of money with our friends in a club ... And I'm not sure our life is actually as nice as it would be if we didn't have such a bullshit job. And didn't do all this harm to the world meanwhile.

I know this is easy to say and hard to do. And like I say, people calling for change always get called hypocrites. The change isn't going to happen if everyone fighting for change is shamed as a hypocrite—but that's the whole idea. The favoured way to close down debate and defend the deadly, the lethal *status quo*—to call anyone who dares think a hypocrite. A hypocrite *pretends* to live up to their ideals. I know I don't live up to my ideals. I see it as a process, of trying to get ever closer, like a limit in maths. If you *can* live up to your ideals, they're not good enough. And if you require people to live up to their ideals instantly, or else you shame them, there's no room to grow. What you're then saying is nobody is allowed to fight the emergency and we all have to sit here and burn. That's the least we could do for the spirit of evil. Because it's not possible to be spotless in a dirty society. So no, it's valid to ask for change before you fully live up to it yourself.

Reforesting the Mind

Susana: We have to work with nature, rather than against it.

Roc: The harm has to stop because if it doesn't stop there's not gonna be any holidays in India. Holidays in India are gonna go. Either because there's no planes because society's collapsed and there are climate refugees from the Horn of Africa or Chelsea living on the runway. Or else because people figure out it's better not to destroy the planet they're living on by flying to India. But they're gonna go, either way. Unless there's some technological advance that we haven't foreseen—which admittedly is the very nature of them. If there is, that will be great, though it will bring other problems. But to *count* on some unexpected technological advance is foolish or dishonest, it's really just a nice excuse to thwart change.

Susana: Reforesting and rewilding are vital, and thank god we have the technology to do the necessary mapping. Recently, I watched a video of a bizarre machine that plants thousands of trees in one second. It's amazing, but I wondered whether the damage to the soil and its dwellers had been taken into account. I watched another video of this actor who plays Iron Man, a superhero determined to save the planet through technology, and he's started up an organisation where he's going to do the same as the superhero he's playing. I found the story fascinating. It also made me think about the hero or heroine's journey, the quest, which is an archetypal theme in storytelling, and how it connects to climate warriors ... Of course, we always have to ask what's the embodied carbon in climate innovation? What are the harmful effects it could bring about? Like diesel was supposed to be better than petrol, and it's much worse. And now, there's talk about geo-engineering, and some people are getting really worried, because it seems it's very much part of the fossil fuel industry.

Roc: Yeah, when you see people talking technological fixes, you find they're really granting themselves permission to go on guzzling fossil fuels, plus do something else imaginary that hasn't been invented yet. And if you want people to develop new technology, one problem is fossil fuels are implicitly subsidised so they're artificially cheap and undercut everything else, when renewables are really much cheaper, if it wasn't for governments and oil & gas being spoilers and doing all they can to keep oil & gas on life support.

Susana: Well, technology is amazing. As a bionic woman, who wears a cochlear implant, I have faith in technology and science. There is a lot of innovation that can add to the collage of measures we were talking about. We need tech fixes, but, yes, we have this problem of blind belief in future technology, as if technology was a religion. We can't put our hopes on the hypothetical tech fix which will save us from ourselves. We have to embrace all our tools. We need low-carbon lifestyles. We have to ration and halt all polluting activities until we come up with non-polluting solutions that re-invent our world.

Becoming Ecological Humans

Roc: We need, unfortunately, no, well maybe fortunately, hardly any cars, hardly any planes. I mean even electric planes and electric cars are harmful because—

Susana: The batteries are harmful.

Roc: The batteries, the embodied carbon, mining, waste. You have to do the calculation to see exactly how harmful they are. Less harmful, but still too harmful for everyone in the world to have one.

Susana: Mm-hmm. We want ethical and sustainable batteries. We do need some cars, some kind of private transport, but certainly not the car nightmare we have at present. As part of the transition, hybrids can be good for city life, or running errands, and car-pooling is a good idea. It's very difficult. I mean, you've seen me with my mother, she's in a wheelchair, and public transport can be very good, but it equally can be very difficult and painfully slow. So, we need different keys for different situations, and there are many situations where you need something that works better than public transport. I mean, like Baker Street station has no disabled access, would you believe it? And I'm finding all the time, lots of stations that have no access for the disabled, which also affects parents carrying buggies. So how do you deal with that? And I'm being London-centric, because in other cities and countries, it's much worse. I was recently in Paris with a wheeled suitcase, and there were no lifts in the main Metro stations I passed through!

Roc: You deal with it with investment and law. But also with an admission that we can't splurge fossil energy all the time without murdering children.

Susana: Investment in these things? That hasn't come forward so far, there are so many stations that don't have access. The process is slow, because public transport is not prioritised.

Roc: Well, it's ... I suspect no new stations are built without access. So that's a start, but it isn't enough. But I think it's similar to what I've already said. It's not a choice between cars or no cars, it's a choice between no cars on the one hand, or no cars and no people on the other. The cars are going to go whatever happens. It's just whether the people go too. I mean, no one can predict the future but, as Thomas Hardy said, sometimes coming events cast a shadow before them. It's looking pretty grim. If we don't find the off-switch to the oil industry and consumerism, vast hordes of us will be swept by hunger across mountains only to walk into guns. I think of Walter Benjamin climbing the Pyrenees, the dye in the nose pads of his glasses bleeding down his face, and on the far side, overdosing on morphine in his cell when told he would be sent back to France. If these times are out of joint, the coming ones are dismembered. Many of us will claim asylum, like Benjamin, in suicide.

Susana: So you don't think electric cars are the answer?

Roc: Possibly part of the transition. Those are really questions of doing the sums and finding out what the reality is. It's like how much embodied carbon is there in an electric car? And in recharging it? Meaning how much CO_2 was emitted in making the car and the electricity.

Susana: We need to build the green industry that produces clean green transport.

Roc: Yes. For instance, there's a company that makes electric quad bikes.

Where I live in the Hebrides, it's eight miles walk to my house from the nearest place I can catch a bus. It's along a track across a mountain to where the little passenger ferry leaves from. And I'm getting older, and if I still live there, there'll come a time when I can't walk. You have to walk in the dark often, in a gale or in a blizzard, so it can be hard. And so, I looked on the internet at electric quad bikes, which are kind of motorbikes with four wheels, that can go over very rough ground. And there's a company in Devon that makes electric quad bikes, and they try and do everything using solar power, and to be low-carbon in their manufacturing of the quad bikes. But you have to look at that sum and see how much fossil fuels have even gone into the making of the machine to make the bikes, and the plastic fairings, and whether a forest was cut down to mine the ore.

Susana: Is that information part of their site, too?

Roc: Some of it. But there's no way round the reality—all this travel is a harmful aberration in the history of humans. The harm has to be discouraged.

Susana: Well, there's the new Ultra Low Emission Zone, the ULEZ.

Roc: But I feel it's window dressing. Because, for instance, it doesn't apply to black cabs, which are the most polluting of all, and usually empty.

Susana: That's unforgivable! If you look at the disabled, they need taxis. Why? Because public transport isn't good enough.

Roc: Yes, but the taxis with their fumes are killing a lot of people, and it's even worse to be dead. Some of the people killed are disabled people. Some are disabled because of the fumes. So public transport has to be good, but above all, we need to travel less.

Susana: But some form of alternative to public transport is necessary. There are new electric taxis, aren't there? All delivery vehicles and taxis should be electric, of course.

Roc: There are some electric taxis, and I think, I can't remember what the rule is, but I think new taxis have to be at least hybrid electric and diesel. The mayor of London has sometimes been accused of window dressing. I think he promised to triple the amount of protected cycle routes by 2020 if he was elected, but hasn't, and he even cancelled some of the ones ready to go like the Westway. And yet he's claiming to have built some huge quantity like 140km or something of cycle infrastructure since taking office. But the previous cycling commissioner, Andrew Gilligan, cycled round it all in February and claims he found the true figure of meaningful new routes proposed and built by the mayor was … zero! He claims there were a lot of signs, a lot of paint, a lot of rebranding of existing routes which were then claimed as new routes, but very little action. I don't know if that's true because I haven't done what he did and cycled all the way round. But there's this whole massive group of people, the cyclists, desperate to stop using so much fossil fuel for transport but to be safeguarded doing so, not to have to risk their lives, and like many others, the mayor seems to be a busy-bee engaged in thwarting them for some fishy reason. Of course the ULEZ is helpful, except perhaps in giving the illusion that something remotely proportionate to the scale of the emergency is being done. It isn't.

Susana: What I see in London—I mean many cities have, especially let's say in the centre, they have pedestrian areas, and London doesn't, really. Because, you know, when there was the TELL THE TRUTH pink boat in Oxford Circus, during the April Rebellion, that was wonderful, and obviously there was no traffic. Pollution went down in London with the Rebellion. It also made me realise, ah, many cities have pedestrianised areas, London doesn't. It's bizarre!

Roc: It's bizarre and sort of very old fashioned and stuck in the past, London, and not adapting.

Susana: Areas like Trafalgar Square could be traffic-free; Oxford Circus. You could have bikes to go up and down the street.

Roc: And Hyde Park could be traffic-free.

Susana: Or you just walk, which is very good for you. It would leave you calm.

Roc: Regent's Park could be traffic-free.

Susana: So, it would be interesting if large areas all over the country would pedestrianise. And not only in the centre. Each borough could have a pedestrianised area, like in villages. Barcelona is pedestrianising large areas in many boroughs. And there's this city, Pontevedra, which has made its historical centre completely car-free. Cities are exclusively built for cars. Most of the space is taken up by cars, marginalising non-car users, as if we were second-class citizens. Non-car users could demand to be equally represented in cities by car-free areas ... I heard in Scotland, they're having traffic-free Mondays.

Roc: Really? I didn't know about that. That's a nice one too, or car-free years.

Susana: So you don't have to visit your family? Yeah! But think about cities like Amsterdam, where most people cycle. There are these free white bikes for public use everywhere. You just pick one up when you need it and leave it when you're finished. It's certainly an example to emulate. There are some interesting changes introduced in some countries, little bitsy bits, and what we need is for it all to be put all together to be effective, so that a real transition starts.

Roc: In London, the white bikes are memorials for cyclists, chained to the place where the cyclist was killed. Yes, I think it will be like a collage, that everyone needs to add something to the collage.

Susana: It could be a collage. It's certainly better than window dressing. Let's hope it becomes a really competitive collage. But the keyword is cooperation. Countries have to start cooperating with each other with the vision that this is our only home.

Polluter Pays or Polluter Steals

Susana: So are you saying, when you do the embedded-carbon maths, that there are no clean green cars?

Roc: A bike is a green car.

Susana: Some people can barely walk or are scared of cycling. The other day I was thinking how to carry things with the least damage to the environment. There are cargo bikes, and electric cargo bikes, which are very expensive. But how do you carry a large canvas, big things?

Roc: Yeah, you roll up your canvas.

Susana: Hm?

Roc: No, our society will have to change.

Susana: We need a change of heart. And we need systemic changes. A car makes carrying things so easy. That's why I asked about the crime against the scientific community. The scientific knowledge about climate change was there since the late 70s, but little has been done, the fact is that renewables could have fully been developed decades ago and, you know, corporations and governments chose not to. Because we could have better technologies for transport and many things, and we haven't because they've been spiked.

Roc: I don't see it exactly like that, I think there are already really good technologies. Like the bicycle, the bicycle is an incredible technology.

Susana: For someone who's fit?

Roc: That's why they are fit, because they have a bike. But for disabled people ... When societies collapse, the disabled people are among the first to go. It's terrifying. So even disabled people have an incentive to change if it helps solve this problem because it's ultra-serious. So that may mean people have to go by bicycle, and disabled people may have to—

Susana: Go on a rickshaw which someone else pedals?

Roc: Good idea! Alternatively, it is an option to go on living like now, temporarily, but then society will collapse. Quite soon, probably. Unless there is an unexpected technological change.

Susana: Electric clean transport and electric cars should be subsidised. Fossil fuel subsidies should go to clean transport. Delivery trucks, lorries and public transport should be all electric, and people should have access to make that change if they need to, because at present people, some of whom have to carry the elderly, can't afford to make the transition from petrol cars to hybrids, let alone electric cars. The cheapest, which are very expensive, are so tiny they can't carry a wheelchair.

Roc: Maybe what we're talking about is more or less damage. So fossil fuel emission is very damaging, maybe electric cars, less damaging. But they may still be too damaging for everyone in the world to have an electric car. That would mean no more nature.

The Problem of Evil: Rampant Consumerism

Susana: The transition has to happen in such a way that the process of making clean electric transport is not harmful either, or else, the harm is minimised. Of course, loads of companies must be thinking about how to do this.

Roc: But possibly consumerism is what is harmful, if it is objects and carbonated energy being consumed. Consuming objects is inherently harmful because they have to be mined and they have to be processed and transported and you have to cut down the forest where the mine is. And the biodiversity emergency will kill us even if the climate doesn't. And so, I think it's more that we do need some objects, we need shelter, we need some clothes and we need to be able to grow food and things like that. And maybe very few people, the people in the privileged West, say, or dictators, could go on acquiring lots of objects and insist no one else can, if they thought they could get away with it. But if everyone is gonna be more equal, then having lots of objects and splurging fossil energy is not consistent with survival.

Susana: There's an obscene surplus of objects. The energy wastage and pollution it generates is astonishing. We can't deal with the surplus. And we can't deal with the waste. We're drowning in it. The outrage people felt when seeing images of the soup of plastic plaguing our oceans and rivers has been effective. Of course, it needs to be more effective. A problem I see with emissions is that they are invisible. We need to make them visible. Produce images that translate the effects of pollutants on the biosphere, so we can visualise what's causing global warming. If we can make images and videos visualising emissions as a soup of colourful plastic objects coming from factories, households, cars, planes, that would have an impact on people. Powerful images of our air, our streets and the sky awash with clouds of plastic, would cause serious understanding and outrage, and trigger new habits and legislation.

Roc: Yeah, it's ridiculous. I think of that quite incredible novel (which risks giving literature a good name) *Philosophical Toys*, where you write about the convertible fetishism of money, and what is essentially the religious significance of shopping. It echoes at a different scale what I say about the religious significance of the motorways. If humans survive, and return to Britain, they will see these great cement slots burnt through the land, and will think they are to do with worship, which is true. They're about, even, human sacrifice: the sacrifice of the walkers, cyclists, of the children whose air was poisoned, of those who will starve when society collapses due to fossil fuels. Glorious horror is the substructure of these shiny cars, which seem to even derange their own drivers when they climb in. To toy with mysticism, a driver is an enraged priest.

Susana: Ha, ha, nice sentence! I love Christian Climate Action. They're doing an excellent job. Some priests genuinely believe their religious way of life will improve humankind! The motorway comes with its own mythology. Especially in America. The motorway as infinity. But I also like your idea of motorways as horizontal sacrificial places, maybe like Aztec pyramids ... Cement is highly polluting. The West causes the destruction that those currently enduring climate change pay for with their lives and livelihoods. Ultimately, we are all sacrificial victims, but some are more than others. The other day I half-watched a documentary about the history of the car on BBC4. Was it propaganda? I found it interesting, that at a time when car use should be rationed until we've made the transition to clean energy, there should be this documentary glorifying the car. I think it briefly mentioned climate change towards the end, without delving into cars' lethal contribution to the predicament we're in, as a way of segueing into the new generation of electric cars, without mentioning embedded carbon. The conclusion was triumphant: 'Cars are here to stay.'

Roc: That's the BBC for you. In *Philosophical Toys* you talk about 'Things that belong to plastic fantastic culture whose fragments end up bursting out of the guts of albatross chicks'. But an electric car, too, is an object, it's a consumer object which people are programmed to think they need.

Susana: There is a problem, which is, many people don't know we're in a Climate Emergency, they don't know the planet is dying on several levels. They don't know how lethal cars are for the environment. And once they know, they don't know how to stop using them, especially if they have to transport heavy stuff and/or access places that can't be reached by public transport. Aviation is another matter, though. Again, many people don't know how lethal flights are for the environment. They don't know that even short-haul flights are deadly. And there is also this wilful blindness. And so, a massive campaign of information and awareness on both fronts is urgent. It must be done on a global scale. We must demand that environmentally sound alternatives are accessible to everyone at an affordable price. How are we going to implement the big lifestyle changes we need?

Volcanic: Twenty Nineteen

Roc: Well, there's another intense Rebellion coming in October. So, yeah. Maybe in that way? There's a lot to look forward to.

Susana: Mmmm, let's hope it's as good! And there's the Global Climate Strike in September. I hear there's a glimmer of hope and our demand to the media to tell the truth is going to be heeded, with lots of media organisations participating.

Roc: Excellent! ... The authorities have a dilemma whether to be ruthless and brutal and try and stop it, or whether to accept it and change, or else hope if they play for time we'll just go away. Now, shall we stop? Would you like to stay for dinner?

Susana: Oh, ok! ... I think XR should train the authorities on climate change. To educate them, or to just say 'This is what's going on. How will you deal with it?'

Roc: By window dressing.

Susana: It's just very difficult, because you know, if they decided to thwart the movement, it could turn very ugly.

Roc: It may turn ugly.

Susana: That's why the Heathrow action is supposed to happen in September as well. It's very important to get it right. I thought maybe we could use beams of black light or dark light to signify pollution, to kind of mimic the lethal vapour trails. I don't know whether beams of black light would interfere with planes. So, that's an idea for an action: the sky awash with dark beams of light.

Roc: That volcano was very effective in Iceland, that stopped all the planes flying.

Susana: I know, I loved that. I've got the pic on my Facebook with the heading: 'Iceland has always managed to surprise me'. I can't remember what the volcano was called.

Roc: The volcano? It was called XR.

Degrowth of Damage

No one can win against kipple. *Philip K. Dick*

Sun and Moon supply their conforming masks, but in this hour of civil twilight all must wear their own faces. *W. H. Auden*

Fossil Fuels Inferno

Roc: The question is to figure out how the trick is done. The news, the lobbying, the rigged education.

Susana: It's appalling that the news is not talking about this unfolding tragedy. Some climate news is covered, but usually only in the environment section, when it should be front-page material. Because I get news through Twitter or Facebook, I don't know where it's placed. Maybe it doesn't matter anymore, because if you follow green social media accounts you get it, but those who mainly watch TV, and BBC News in particular, are in limbo. And that is a problem.

We should all know how lethal fossil fuels are. Greta Thunberg said in her speech yesterday in Australia, what many of us have been saying: 'How come this is not front-page news?' There's a lot of fragmentation with ecological collapse and biodiversity destruction coverage. We're hearing so many hundred dead dolphins or whales have washed up in this or that country. All these different species are dying, all over the world, all the time. Sometimes, the coverage is there, but it's there in a way that doesn't give you the full picture. There are all these mass animal die-offs that are reported as a 'mystery'. The media presents this terrible news as isolated events, without digging into the cause.

Roc: Well, there's a very good reason for that, which is that then we might do something about it. There are forces in society that don't want us to do anything about it.

Susana: Which forces would you say they are?

Roc: Well, the fossil fuel industry. Nobody knows exactly how much they are spending to ensure they can continue with their murder spree. It's said it's something like a billion dollars a year spent on manipulating public perception of climate disaster. And they pay for politicians in the US, and UK politicians are paid for and UK parties are bought. So, a huge amount of money goes into manipulating public perception of reality, and manipulating politics, and it's a complete tragedy.

Chronicle of Climate Chaos Foretold ... by ExxonMobil

Susana: And of course, how can we expect the mainstream media to be transparent about climate and ecological collapse, and the sweeping changes needed, when it depends on advertising, most of which sells us high-carbon lifestyles: cars, holidays, cruises, useless products. Fossil fuel companies do know that what they're doing is monstrous. Because the research has been there for decades. And they've been trying to either bury that research or deny it altogether. They knew emissions damaged the environment in the fifties and sixties. They knew fossil fuels caused global warming since 1977. Around that time one of ExxonMobil's employees, James Black, wrote an internal briefing, 'The Greenhouse Effect', which warned human-caused emissions could raise global temperatures and result in serious consequences and urged changes in energy strategies.

In fact, it was known way before. Interestingly, this scientist and women's rights campaigner called Eunice Foote discovered the greenhouse effect in 1856. Her discovery was presented, and then, mentioned in Scientific American. Like many women scientists, she was erased from history, until a decade ago. John Tyndall carried out more developed experiments in 1859. So, the science has been there since the nineteenth century.

Roc: Yeah. It's appalling. It's not the greenhouse effect, it's the sauna effect. And a sauna with us bolted inside.

Susana: In the States this fossil fuel company has just been rebranded as Freedom Gas.

Roc: Yes. And Voldemort, aka BP, changed its logo to look like a flower. They all make a big thing about their renewable operations, but they're often something like one quarter percent of their total operations, and it's window dressing. Like the governments, they all like window dressing. They like pretending they're doing something but actually not doing anything significant at all. They like it because it works, because people are gullible and can be manipulated.

Susana: Culture's very good at whitewashing and greenwashing.

Roc: Like the British Museum, you mean?

Susana: Exactly. And the National Portrait Gallery.

Roc: Yes. BP sponsors the National Portrait Gallery. Well, I had a funny experience because I was taken to, I think it was the BP dinner, when they chose the best portrait of the year. And there was a fancy dinner in the National Portrait Gallery, and everyone was sitting at these little tables of eight people wearing evening dress and black ties. And for some reason they put me on the table with kind of the head of BP, the second in charge of BP, BP's top lawyer, and their partners. So, there were six of them and my friend and me. And I said what I thought about the mess, the disaster, the tragedy we are in, and it was as if I'd hurt their feelings, and that I was behaving in a boorish way. They'd bought me dinner, and I was dissing them.

Susana: So maybe you were put there for a purpose.

Roc: Yeah. I didn't talk to them in a hostile way at all, I wanted to understand their psychology and how they saw it. But in a way, they didn't see it. Something had happened in their minds that they didn't see what they were doing, and they must have thought, 'Who's this rude jerk who's talking about horror?' I wasn't asked back.

Susana: They were offended because they know. Maybe it's just shamelessness, mixed in with wishful thinking. And they're in denial, or partly in denial. I mean how can you be in denial about this? You can't.

Roc: Well, it's true. And also, if they're fixing campaigns of climate deniers, they must know. There is a problem with propaganda in general which is that if you're organising propaganda, which the fossil fuel industry does, you sometimes start believing it yourself. Like Hitler, I don't know if you know this, but Hitler spent a lot of the war in something he called 'The Wolf's Lair' which was this complex of concrete bunkers in what's now Poland. And there was so much propaganda about Germany winning the war and things like that. And then I think in late 1944, he flew back to Berlin, and he looked out of the aeroplane and he saw that Berlin was rubble. And he didn't know. Nobody had told him. He was devastated. He'd believed the propaganda that he himself had ordered. So, it could be they believe their own propaganda. But that's becoming harder and harder.

Susana: With some of the green Twitter accounts that I follow, sometimes they are stalked by a BP-promoted tweet about their green projects, which is utter rubbish. They have a campaign of stalking lots of green accounts to greenwash their image, telling you things that you know are not true. I just read something that condemns BP completely and utterly, and BP stalks with their investment in renewables, though I haven't seen them stalking Greenpeace! I've seen it with XR.

Roc: I'm sure BP would love to sponsor XR.

Susana: That would be interesting. That would be a very happy marriage. Yeah. But the oil industry lobbying must stop. I mean, for capitalism to have access to governments the way it does, it's outrageous really. Abhorrent. And tragic.

Roc: It is a terrible tragedy. Yeah. But don't forget most oil is pumped by states—usually the state owns the means of production wholly, which is state socialism, or if not then partially, as in Western oligarchies. And a first step in redeeming that tragedy is transparency. Like if you put it all in public what is happening, and name the organisations doing it.

Susana: Well, we don't have that transparency. You can read articles here and there where corruption is revealed, usually in *Double Down News* and *Open Democracy*, because it tends not to be part of the mainstream. XR, Greenpeace, *EcoHustler* and all the environmental publications are fierce in exposing ecological vandalism. Exposure is vital, but little or nothing seems to be done about corruption.

Roc: Yeah. It's wicked, and it's how, say in Britain, the party system works, with donors to the party and the peers. There's a good book called *The Prostitute State* by Donnachadh McCarthy, who was something like deputy chair of the Liberal Democrats. So, he saw from the inside how the Liberal Democrat peers were usually sponsored by a nuclear company or a fossil fuel company and the same with other parties, the Labour Party and the Conservative Party. And in that way, and by political donations, and by seconding experts to government departments, and by funding thinkthanks, industry would control the legislature and thwart people trying to avert the climate disaster.

Susana: It's blood money. And it's not only the blood of our children. Let's not forget that in some countries the oil industry has worked hand in hand with the military to displace Indigenous populations, resulting in Indigenous activists being killed. It's soul-destroying. Also, some governments that are not directly involved turn a blind eye to the murdering of Indigenous activists. This is particularly the case with deforestation. Something has to be done to protect activists.

Science and Humanity Divide

Roc: Another thing that's given rise to this tragedy in Britain, at least, is that education has been artificially separated into the humanities and the sciences, and that means society is divided. It means few people have the training to see the whole picture.

Susana: Well, scientists would do.

Roc: Scientists have got the training to understand, but they're also trained not to be protestors because you're supposed to be objective, record, describe, but not intervene. And also, scientists are often not good communicators. The scientists know but can't tell, and the humanities crew can tell but don't know.

Susana: There's a missing link there because if a scientist is actually recording all this devastating data as part of their research ... How long can they keep quiet about it?

Roc: Scientists are becoming protestors now because of the horrific situation we are facing, but so far scientists have been conditioned not to be protestors and are having to overcome that conditioning. But there's another problem: scientists are not trained to communicate well because that allegedly belongs in the humanities. And journalists tend to be people from the humanities who are not trained in science. There are many counterexamples, but in general, if you read what journalists write, even on internal evidence, you can see they lack an understanding of statistics or they're not that numerate. We're lucky if they're literate.

Susana: Well, for a lay reader the language can be alienating. I had to look up many concepts when reading about climate change. Sometimes there are scientific arguments which are complex.

Roc: Yeah. And that's the essence. Journalists are the single largest sector whose failure has got us into this mess—apart perhaps from teachers. And accountants. And politicos. And bankers. And insurers. Actually, when you start pointing the finger, you run out of fingers. And you've got to save one to point at yourself. And perhaps it's not the journalists at fault so much as the editors. Actually, the owners. So I should say, the media is the single largest sector. And it's the nature of modern mainstream journalism that you have to be processing really fast because there aren't enough journalists and you aren't paid enough, and you don't have time to go deep. But unfortunately, we need deep understanding to solve the problems because the problems are deep and complicated—and wrapped in layers of propaganda—most journalism is regurgitated press releases from governments or businesses. So that, even if the journalists were to get on top of it—and there are signs they are beginning to now—the editors won't let it through and the readership don't have the concepts we need to get it, and besides, we're obsessed with murderers, influencers and It-people and don't have time for the end of the world.

Susana: Fastness can be a curse, as there is no time to finesse the detail and accuracy is often sacrificed. There are so many people writing for specialised publications, whereas someone who works as a journalist has to churn out articles all the time. The main thing they have is a platform for their voice to be projected.

Roc: Ideally you need to re-fuse the scientific education and the humanities education. They've been separated partly to level the playing field for children who find either science or the humanities a challenge. Or even for the teachers who do. It's an equity play. That's generous, but also misguided, because it means your civilisation collapses, which is even worse for the challenged.

Frugality, Cats and Utopia

Roc: Would you like more cider, Susana? If I went and got another bottle?

Susana: You are not drinking at all.

Roc: I am drinking.

Susana: I am going to become more and more incoherent.

Roc: How will I tell? No but seriously, I drank half of that bottle.

Susana: Did you.

Roc: Yes.

Susana: Ok.

Roc: We are talking very much about Britain; it is local, what we are saying.

Susana: I know in Barcelona, there's a strong XR movement. And then, talking to Catalonian friends, I realised that it's not in the mainstream media at all! Same when I went to Paris recently. So, I know XR keeps on growing and growing, but wonder whether the media in those countries are reporting on it.

Roc: And this is such a big problem, that we need many, many different ways of solving it, and XR is only one. And perhaps it's suited to Britain and less well suited to more physically repressive regimes. Like in Saudi Arabia, or Russia, it couldn't work so well, because you wouldn't live long enough to achieve anything. This is obviously a world-wide problem, and there are people who have been fighting and dying for many years all over the world trying to solve it in ultra-difficult situations because there are many, many repressive regimes. And people are still being environmentalists and risking their lives. And in the UK so far—and it may change—people aren't risking their lives. We're risking our freedom but not our lives. We're in the UK right now, and we're talking in a UK-centric way. But there's incredible stuff happening all over the world.

Susana: Yes, but in some places it's hardly possible.

Roc: So, we need not only protest, but research, education, feminism—because feminism reduces natality and after consumerism, a part of the problem is the earth's carrying capacity. We need—

Susana: That's why I decided to have three cats.

Roc: But the population of cats—

Susana: Because they're better. They have a much lower carbon footprint.

Roc: The population of cats is going up too. We need frugality, a guzzling approach to asceticism. Lots of books, lots of music, lots of singing, dancing, lots of massages, lots of therapy.

Susana: You're talking about Utopia.

Roc: And—

Susana: Will be good to have that.

Costa Rica, Cuba, Bolivia and Ecuador Lead the Way

Susana: Going back to what you were saying about talking in a UK-centric way and incredible stuff happening all over the world, Costa Rica is very interesting ecologically. Since 2014, it has been generating more than 98% of its electricity from renewable sources. It has a successful reforestation project and it has just declared that it plans to ban and eliminate fossil fuels by 2021.

Roc: Fantastic! On the other hand it has a business model based partly on jet-set tourism ...

Susana: Yes, that's Costa Rica's Achilles heel, and it seems they're working on it. There are campaigns that encourage tourists to be carbon neutral, buy bona fide carbon offsets, and stay as green as possible. One of the essays I have to mark at the Open University is on Costa Rica's ecotourism. The lethal carbon footprint of flights is the problem. Ultimately ecotourists should know better. Latin America has very strong environmental movements. Unfortunately, it also has the highest rate of murders of environmental activists ... At the April

Rebellion, I spoke to a guy who was giving out leaflets about Cuba and the environment. He gave me a leaflet about the Earth Summit in Rio de Janeiro in 1992, with a speech by Castro. Castro was already strongly denouncing consumer societies as chiefly responsible for the appalling environmental destruction we are seeing. He was denouncing the poisoning of rivers, land, air, and how, you know, Cuba didn't want to follow that kind of suicidal route.

Roc: And did he succeed? I mean is there evidence that Cuba is less damaged in its environment?

Susana: I followed up on this. And Cuba comes very close to sustainable development at high Human Development Index (HDI). The journalist Jason Hickel speaks about how, unfortunately, there are no countries which have sustainable development at very high HDI, which measures life expectancy, education, and per capita income. He goes on to criticise the necessity of the per capita income indicator. If you remove it, Costa Rica and Cuba come at the top of sustainable development. He's devising a Sustainable Development Index, which, of course, will recognise the North as tragically underdeveloped. Cuba is also a leading country in reforestation. Obviously, there's a lot of recycling.

Roc: Yeah. And degrowth. I mean Castro achieved degrowth! Though to be fair, the States helped out.

Susana: Though I was thinking about all these ancient cars that really pollute.

Roc: That's true.

Susana: But I should think generally the attitude is more about wellbeing and sustainability, and less about economic growth ... Cuba has recently enshrined the fight against climate change in its constitution. Ecuador's constitution is regarded as the most ecologically aware legal system in the world ... Latin America has the second lowest greenhouse emissions in the world. And in many Latin American countries where they have Indigenous people, they have inherited the local knowledge about nature, and Bolivia has Mother Earth laws, which grant all nature equal rights to humans.

Roc: I love Latin America, and several of my dearest friends were born there. I was lucky enough to spend some time there with them when I was young and it was the happiest time of my life. But I'm sceptical of some of your claims. The Mother Earth laws are fantastic and much needed, but they have to actually work. Bolivia has a good reputation for this, and perhaps Ecuador. But I suspect the Amazon countries, in burning the rainforest, have some of the highest carbon emissions in the world. And even if not, they are systematically annihilating biodiversity at a scale which is risking all our lives and may well kill us. Annihilating, too, many Indigenous Amazon people—I've met some of them, who came to ask our help, and they left me in no doubt about the horror of what was going on. And Cuba—I've never been there, I'd love to go and spend time there if I could find someone sailing there, so perhaps I don't know enough about it. But again, I find myself being suspicious of the claims you are making for it—especially given my experience of other socialist societies—they typically find it hard to motivate people, and therefore in every single one where I have direct experience they've had to use violence on ordinary people. Psychiatric hospitals for the sane (that happened to my friend Igor), labour camps, being forced into the army, etc. If Castro really has made things better for people than they would otherwise be, it may be a first for an authoritarian socialist regime, and maybe there's a lot to be learned in that case. Venezuela, too, I have been there briefly, I loved it, but it's not going that well at the moment, tragically. Perhaps these regimes are less horrific than the non-socialist authoritarian regimes, I don't know—a body count would be a good proxy—but I'm sceptical about the idea that authoritarianism and totalitarianism can ever be pleasant. I suppose the argument in their favour is that there are places where the alternative is disorder, which is even worse.

NIMBY & the Disconnect of City Cultures

Susana: In the Global South, ecology is a concern that is closer to the heart than in Europe.

Roc: I'd say it's close to the heart in Europe too. I mean, in a city maybe not, but I live in the country, and yes, I'm part of nature. So, I think perhaps what you're describing is that city cultures all over the world are disconnected. And perhaps rural cultures are connected all over the world because you have to be, if you're working, say on the land, you have to understand nature. It doesn't work if you don't understand nature. I suppose it works if you have machinery and fossil fuel fertilisers and pesticides and can import masses of soya based feed grown where there used to be rainforest. But possibly you have to understand nature even to use your pesticides properly—to exterminate it efficiently. And then, even in cities, the cyclists are connected to nature, the dog-owners. Those who can see the river or the clouds.

Susana: Good point about the disconnect of city cultures. You live on a deserted island. How did that come about? And what made you want to go off-grid?

Roc: Like many people, wildness is important to me. And I'd lived in various places where I saw the nature and wildness being destroyed and I didn't have the resources to stop it. And I tried to think where it's not going to happen. I was really looking for somewhere I could protect. Like, people make fun of NIMBY, which stands for not in my back yard, where people are trying to protect their own little area of suburb or of rainforest from a bypass or a gold mine, but I think NIMBY is a positive force, is our only hope, and that if everyone could protect their own area … People make fun of that and say nimbies are selfish spoilsports because they don't want a motorway in their garden or their rainforest to be torched. They say, too, incidentally, what's it got to do with you if the place you are trying to protect is not your back yard—the Amazon for instance. Which is a glib way of saying you are not entitled to fight for anywhere—your own locality or other people's. So, anyway, I was looking for a backyard I could protect. And I found this deserted island, called Gometra, and I was fortunate enough to be able to raise the money to buy it.

Susana: When was that?

Roc: Nearly thirty years ago. So, I went to live there with my first child. I misjudged how difficult it would be because there's no doctor. There's no school. There's no ferry. For much of the time there was no way of contacting the outside world, and so it was incredible and beautiful, but it was also quite difficult and, with hindsight, dangerous. And so, I went there to live, but I ended up living there part-time because it was too hard to bring up children in that environment full time. Even if the High Court had allowed me to be there full time, which it didn't, I would have wanted there to be other children to play with. I didn't want mine to only know each other.

Susana: Of course, because it must be quite isolating. Really beautiful and amazing, but.

Roc: Yeah. It's pure nature with hardly any humans, and ideally you need humans *and* nature to be happy. A kind of urban wilderness, or rural city, is the ideal.

Susana: So, what about micronations and Gometra, the idea of starting up a micronation because then you would get people?

Roc: We would, and there is an island quite near us called the Isle of Man which is a micronation and is full of people. The problem for somewhere like Gometra is we belong to the United Kingdom, and so all the rules are made to benefit the United Kingdom or Scotland and not to benefit us. The currency is set, the interest rates, the exchange rate, all for the kind of societies that are on the mainland. And the result of that is to suck resources out of places which have lower productivity because of their natural economic disadvantages, like remoteness and lack of infrastructure, and to suck people out in effect. So yeah, I'd be very in favour of independence and being a micronation. I think we could do an amazing job. Only, we might need to free-ride on NATO because otherwise the Chinese or the Russians would snap us up and introduce their political arrangements which are even more horrific than ours. If body counts are how you judge.

Degrowth of Damage

Susana: With Brexit on the menu, do you think if Scotland became independent it would find it easier to flourish?

Roc: The Scottish government is very business-friendly. As I've said, the salmon farms off the West Coast of Scotland are a complete disaster for biodiversity. They're killing the wild salmon. And in the Scottish government, there are regulatory bodies—Scottish Natural Heritage, Scottish Environmental Protection Agency, Marine Scotland Science—which are supposed to protect the sea, but they're not succeeding. And the Scottish government has the project of doubling the amount of salmon produced in these farms. So, I'm not optimistic about the

Scottish government being helpful. They think about money and headlines and votes, and not about biodiversity. They talk about it, but the outcome is extinction and damage.

Susana: Yesterday I read that the prime minister of New Zealand, Jacinda Ardern, an amazingly inspiring woman, has declared a budget for wellbeing and her government's policies are going to be shaped according to wellbeing rather than GDP. She talks about climate change as her generation's 'nuclear-free moment'.

Roc: Excellent.

Susana: And hopefully many other countries will follow because that's what has to happen. The social contract is broken on so many levels: rampant inequality, racism, ecocide. There is a common denominator to our woes: greed. We need a budget for wellbeing, and we need to abandon our current ideas about GDP. It is insufficient and unethical as an index for development. Her proposal, and that's what many environmentalists have been insisting on, is about degrowth.

Roc: I agree entirely about the wellbeing. I think there is a question about how you define wellbeing, because one person's wellbeing is not another person's wellbeing. And some people might define it as watching *Love Island* 24 hours a day, and others might define it as listening to their friend playing the guitar. So how you define it is important, but wellbeing is the right thing to try to measure and deliver. What I disagree about is degrowth, because you can have endless growth in massages and low-carbon food and your friend playing the guitar and writing and reading books.

Susana: We could turn half the planet into a library, and the other half into a massage parlour? No, seriously ... Now, when we talk about degrowth we talk about degrowth of the industries that are harming the planet. We're talking about those industries that need to change, or disappear.

Roc: Then I agree. When you mentioned GDP, the GDP can go up, but it has to be going up in terms of massages and low-carbon food and books. That's all I'm saying.

Susana: Well, that would be good, but it won't happen that way.

Roc: To say degrowth is a bit misleading. What we need is degrowth, as you say, of damage. And that I agree with entirely. But there's a lot of people who say that GDP has to shrink. It actually is shrinking now but people don't realise that because of rigged accounting, but it doesn't have to shrink. It can increase, if you are only honest in your measurement. Because what is presented as economic growth now is not actual growth: the destruction of value in burning the fossil fuels and destroying the rainforest is artificially kept off the balance sheet. It's sick, it's such an obvious ruse, but more or less all of us are taken in. The macro-economists working on national accounts, the accountants and auditors working on company accounts, with their obscuring of these effects, are helping enable the end of the world and the slaughter of their own children. It couldn't be sicker. This is pollution in the realm of knowledge. It's what's called a negative sum game.

Zero Sum Game

Susana: I like the way you put it: non-sustainable accountancy is pollution in the realm of knowledge. We have to, of course, challenge accountancy.

Roc: If you go further, and not just account for, but progressively internalise the negative economic externalities, make people pay for their pollution, so people actually have to pay through the nose for the damage they want to cause, and ideally can be paid for their efforts to fix it, there will be a massive rebalancing of the economy into a more efficient state where value is no longer destroyed. More massages and books and music and non-fossil-fuel-based food and renewables and passive houses and forestry and peatbogs—*and* a better redistributive safety net—and we can have real, not phoney, economic growth. So, I don't buy the whole degrowth argument. But it's a quibbling about misleading words, what I call the propaganda model of language, plus a mathematical intuition, this, because I haven't done the sums. And, true, degrowth of damage may not feel like economic growth because we are drunk on fossil fuels, and equate guzzling them with growth. So, we have to kick that addiction.

And meanwhile, with our phoney accounts, we fall into the trap Hayek, if I remember rightly which can never be relied on, identified and which Keynes, just before he died, wrote to Hayek to affirm. And this is because if your pricing signals are subverted by the false accounting of the macro-economists and the accountancy profession, then you are operating a de facto semi-command economy, which is impossible to do with any efficiency in allocation of your resources. You end up destroying value. Right now, the world can't afford to squander any efficiency, while still feeding and sheltering everyone and simultaneously repairing biodiversity.

I've seen it first-hand, in the Soviet Union, which controlled the biggest territory of any state in the world, with a modest population, and yet couldn't feed everyone well because of the difficulty of doing so with a command economy—with big government, in effect. So, in Soviet Russia, I was often hungry. I would queue for hours out in the blizzard and end up with two pasties about the size of snail shells, one for me and one for my friend K.

Susana: The idea of what constitutes wealth must be transformed. Our economy has to be re-invented. Our culture has to be re-imagined. Yet again, it's a question of integrity, honesty and telling the truth, because at present, yes, 'growth' is a negative-sum game. So, let's dispel the growth myth. Let's emphasise that growth isn't such. The concept should include social justice too, both related and unrelated to climate change. Well, various kinds of injustice and inequality cross over each other, and we can see this clearly with climate justice.

June 2019 Dialogue: Ratatouille Rendezvous

Ratatouille Rendezvous

> What our children have to fear are not the cars on the freeways of tomorrow, but our own pleasure in calculating the most elegant parameters of their deaths. *J. G. Ballard*

Rebel Palace, 8th June, 2019.

'Would you like some cider, Susana?' 'Yes, please, I like that it isn't too sugary ... Where do you buy it?' 'Online.'

Carbon's Dividend and the Problem of Evil

Susana: Let's focus on solutions.

Roc: The question is how to discourage the activity that's doing the damage. And to provide alternative activities which ideally, begin to repair it—so we can leave this borrowed planet better than we found it. There are different ways to discourage harmful behaviour. You can criminalise it or penalise it in civil law—this is the idea of ecocide and related ideas. You can price it—so that people have to pay the cost of what they are doing. The proceeds can be divided up to go towards a universal basic income, or to pay for healthcare or other social goods, like paying for the energy transition in the Global South. The cost is so high that the damage would effectively stop, so ultimately there wouldn't be much coming in. I have heard someone say that an Amazonian burger priced at its true cost would be approximately $36,000 which sounds like an underestimate. Or you can undercut it—even ignoring the cost of the damage they do, few coal-fired power stations are economically viable even now—they are just kept going out of inertia, political capture and the desire to preserve jobs. And finally, there are social toxification and moral exhortation. All of these mechanisms are well understood. We will need them all. The problem is political and social—how to get them adopted—it's not a problem of engineering or economics.

Susana: That's a massive problem, and can we separate fields just like that? We have to embrace all the alternatives. 'Alternative' may be a keyword as the old guard is deeply entrenched in its old harmful ways. Fortunately, many people, collectives and initiatives try to critique and bypass our current system, but the political establishment is enmeshed with unethical and dodgy economics. The dictatorship of capital ruthlessly rules politics, and to various extents, our lives. The question is how to move beyond the socio-economic systems that ravage our biosphere, that's to say, all the ecosystems, how to forge a socially just and sustainable world. We want a system where we decide where our taxes go … On things we can do on a personal level you recently mentioned the necessity of getting rid of cars. How would you go about it?

Roc: I would make cars so expensive that everyone wanted to spend their money on books instead.

Susana: But people already have cars.

Roc: Well, I'd make buying the petrol so expensive. Yeah. And I would give that money back to the people in cash. If I had a choice, I could either have a car and drive to the country on the weekend, and pay like thousands to do so—probably still only a fraction of its true cost in terms of damage to everyone's children including my own. And if I did drive to the country and paid thousands, the government would take that money and divide it up into equal shares and give it back to everyone. So, instead of driving, I could get my share of the drivers' thousands, and I could spend it on something else that wasn't harmful and probably also more exciting than sitting in a smelly tin box spoiling everyone's fun. It's the citizens' dividend, as it were, so that the money the government takes from people who want to pollute is shared out among everyone, or it's given to poor people, or it's spent on the NHS. That's a political decision, but it comes back. I think then I wouldn't drive to the country, because there are things I'd rather do with that much money.

Susana: That's an interesting idea. But which government do you envisage doing that?

Roc: Well, a carbon price, which is what we're talking about, is not going to happen without a carbon dividend, which is the money coming back. No government will succeed in putting an effective carbon price in unless the money is returned to the people. The money has to come back because people won't vote for it otherwise, despite what's being done to their children by the polluters. Most of us care more about money than harm.

Susana: Some people call cars death machines ... I don't know whether it's too much cider or ...

Roc: Or not enough cider! What I'm saying is, you know the way 97 per cent of climate scientists say climate collapse is happening and it's caused by humans. So likewise, if you look at economists, most economists say, the way to solve this problem, in the quickest way with the least amount of human suffering, and famine, and all the other things that happen when there's a severe economic disruption, is by having a pollution price or a pollution fee or a pollution tax, whatever you want to call it.

Of course economists have a bad reputation, and rightly so, but on this I think they are right. What happens when someone drives a car is that they are getting the benefit, which is driving, and everyone else is getting the cost, which is greenhouse gas pollution and their lungs not working anymore. And their intelligence being stunted. And getting cancer and dementia. What happens at the moment, is the people causing the damage are not paying for the damage—they are stealing from everyone else. The idea of the carbon price is that if you want to harm everyone's children, you have to stop stealing and pay for it. And if you have to pay for it you don't like that and you stop doing it. It's not much fun anyway, is it? I sometimes feel we're just going through the motions, flying back and forth everywhere—and sleeping in departure lounges on piles of luggage containing stuff we don't even need, when our flights are cancelled.

All these tools exist, the economics are well understood, and they're effective. In Britain there is a carbon price which is set at about £20 for a tonne of CO_2, I think. It's just not nearly high enough, it has to move steadily higher each year. To avoid an abrupt economic shock which disrupts food growing, for instance, but so that carbon emissions are rapidly discouraged and sink to zero. And I believe it's also rigged right now by the free issuing of carbon credits to polluters. That bit has to end. It's like QE in the realm of pollution—except unconditional QE is really QE in the realm of pollution too.

And in Britain there's no explicit carbon dividend yet—the carbon dividend is what makes it politically palatable, because people are much more willing to pay a carbon price if they see the money is coming back to them as some kind of universal basic income. And the carbon dividend is given to the polluters at present. The problem is a political one, which is that electorates keep voting for governments who don't want to solve the problem because they've been bought by oil & gas or other vested interests. And many voters are brainwashed by the media and the education system, and the education of many voters is such that most haven't been taught to second-guess the media, or understand the science. The way the media carry on reminds me of a scene in one of the Jason Bourne films where all the CCTVs turn demurely away for someone to be murdered. Except in this case it's everyone—everyone turning away, and everyone being murdered. So, there's a political and educational and media problem, but I don't think there's an economic problem or an engineering problem. It's difficult, but very doable. The political one is the real difficulty, and that is what XR is addressing. Making, as Rupert Read said, the politically impossible politically possible. And as I say, going further—making it politically necessary.

Ecocide

Susana: Shouldn't this kind of harm just be criminalised? It's almost like, if you want to murder someone, you pay a tax, or a bribe, which is what some companies do anyway. I'm really interested in the concept of ecocide. And in the reality of, you know, we're part of the natural living world, and pollution is killing people. The numbers are vast—worldwide there are 8.8 million early deaths a year. It's killing the planet. What are we doing about that? Environmental destruction in all its guises should be made a crime, all these harmful, disgusting industrial activities and criminal polluters have to be prosecuted, they have to stop doing what they are doing, because they are destroying the climatic system on which we all depend. As part of the transition, we have to have other measures like, maybe a creation of lots of traffic-free areas, car-free days, car-rationing, all sorts of ways to reduce traffic drastically. Electric cars should be made way cheaper. And they should be produced ethically and sustainably.

Roc: But I think there's an inconsistency in what you're saying. Like I agree with you. I think there's three things here. One is the existing laws that we have now, which people are breaking, and they need to be enforced. For instance, expanding Heathrow...

Susana: Mmmm—

Roc: ... violates laws about the Paris Agreement-style targets because it's against the law to expand Heathrow in my view, without further explanation of how this is compatible with existing UK climate obligations—the Climate Change Act, the Paris Agreement. But, the judiciary is not energetically enforcing those laws yet, so it looks like Heathrow may expand. So, there's the existing laws that have to be used properly and one of our many jobs is to encourage the judiciary to use them properly.

Then there's new laws, and ecocide is this brilliant proposal by Polly Higgins as you say, that you have a law which makes what she calls 'ecocide'—the destruction of an ecosystem which humans depend on—a crime against humanity, like a war crime. So, that's a powerful idea. A beautiful idea. And it has to happen. It has to happen as quickly as possible. But it's not going to happen easily, because extremely powerful people stand to lose out. And remember too, that war crimes still happen, and it takes years to prosecute them even if you catch the suspect. While a carbon price is instant.

And then what is also needed is a way to transform this society from where it is now into where it needs to be. And that can't happen like an immediate jump. If you brake too hard you skid and/or everyone goes through the windscreen. XR has said it could take six or seven years. So, the best way to transform is with a carbon price because it can be steadily raised, to avoid the kind of economic heart-attack solutions which lead to famine and social disorder and authoritarianism of left or right.

XR doesn't have an explicit demand around avoiding famine, but I think it's fair to say it's implicit. If right now you said no fossil fuels can be used anymore, from this instant, there would be starvation because farms are using fossil fuels to produce wheat and rice we are all eating. Very quickly the carbon price has to rise over the six-year period or however long, because we don't know how long we've got. It might be too late already. We might have ten years, but we really have to move fast to have the best chance. Because as I keep saying, the choice is not between having fossil fuel cars and not having them. The choice is between no cars on the one hand, and no cars and no people on the other. There aren't going to be fossil cars either way. The choice we've got is whether we go too, as well as the cars, or whether we stay on without them. So even if it's unpleasant and difficult, which it may be for all of us, it has to happen. Unless, of course, there is some staggering technological breakthrough like fusion, or else most people die and the few that are left go on sitting in their traffic jams which apparently turns them on in some twisted way.

Susana: Fusion might happen, but not fast enough. We have to act immediately. But how can the sense of urgency be conveyed when our governments and the media are not willing to put the stark truth out there?

Roc: By occupying Waterloo Bridge and having a festival and a thousand arrests that the media have to report. And then 50,000 people join XR and many of them are willing to be arrested in turn. So that's the way change can happen and has to happen. The brilliant and brave people who design actions such as the taking of Waterloo Bridge cannot be credited, for fear of reprisal, but it may turn out we owe them almost everything.

Gandhi & Urgent Transitions

Susana: We need urgent transitions.

Roc: The carbon price is a way of calculating the transition pathway in the least destructive way possible. By destructive, I mean least suffering, human, animal, vegetable. And the price also amounts to an ecocide law de facto. Because say you want to kill someone: you're running a fossil fuel company or you're driving a black cab or something, and you want the right to kill someone by emitting your nanoparticles. If you're going to pay the full cost of that, that cost is huge. Like how much are you going to have to pay to kill someone? Monsanto has just lost a case in the United States. These two people who used Monsanto RoundUp weedkiller and they think they got cancer from that and the court has decided they probably did, and it put a fine on Monsanto of $2 billion.

And Monsanto is worth about $60 billion and it has probably killed a ton of people. Just a few days ago another court dropped it to $86 million, but that is still a disincentive to a company like Monsanto, given how many thousands of times they may have to pay it. Of course they'll buy politicians and prosecutors to wriggle out of it—that's the whole problem. But I'm saying where the true cost is rigorously imposed on the people who want to kill people, they'll go out of business really quickly. They will stop. It amounts to a similar thing, using a different mechanism, to making a crime of ecocide. Though you could argue it's more effective more quickly—war crimes still take place despite the Hague Conventions. So we need both belt and braces.

Susana: We need accountability, we need to multiply litigation, we need legislative changes. What I was saying before is, what kind of governments will implement these laws because the governments we have are for the most part complicit or are part of a racket or they are being lobbied by these companies and they're part of the same thing. Fast inaction ...

Roc: Can I answer that with a question?

Susana: Mmmm.

Roc: What sort of government would withdraw from India?

Susana: From India?

Roc: Yeah. India was part of the British Empire. Gandhi and his followers decided it shouldn't be. They won, the British withdrew. What has to happen now is something like that. More cider, Susana?

Susana: Yes, please ...! Yeah, civil disobedience ... Gandhi foresaw the problem of global industrialisation. There's this quote where he equates it with locusts, let me google it ... Here it is, it's from 1928: 'God forbid that India should ever take to industrialism after the manner of the West. If an entire nation of 300 million took to similar economic exploitation, it would strip the world bare like locusts.'

Roc: There is another school of thought that it should be achieved by rationing, everyone gets an allocation of fossil fuels they can burn. Well, if they can sell their ration, that probably equates to a carbon price plus dividend model, and could be a politically palatable way to package a carbon price. But if they can't sell it, many people are just going to guzzle stuff they don't really want, just to use up their ration. While other people—farmers for instance—won't be able to access the fuels they need to transition.

Susana: The idea of fossil fuel rationing is interesting and doable. And of course, it has to be implemented in a rational way, so that farmers are able to transition. Lots of different ideas and strategies should be tried out simultaneously. Attack the fossil fuel beast from all sides! That's the strategy we need. Back to being charged for polluting, when you book a flight now, you can pay an extra £1 to offset carbon emissions. £1!

Roc: I mean, do you believe everyone? They're lying.

Susana: Exactly.

Roc: It's like recycling or ...

Susana: I was recently feeling very frustrated about recycling. Because I try to recycle everything, repurpose, upcycle, re-use everything. It's very time-consuming. Like I keep some things I think I can repurpose, and in the end, it just becomes impossible. We have so much kipple, people throw away so many things into the street, and it's complete excess everywhere ... in so-called wealthy societies. Recently, I read that tons of unsold clothes are regularly buried. The fashion industry is lethal! The Ellen MacArthur Foundation has estimated the emissions from making textiles were 1.2 billion tonnes of CO_2-equivalent in 2015! More than all international flights and maritime shipping combined. And this is supposed to rise! ... Something that makes me seethe too is the idea of humans being paid for designing certain parts of a product so that it breaks. Often, you can't find spares, so that's more kipple for the landfill. Planned obsolescence should be banned across the world. And repair workshops should proliferate. Let's revamp billboards with Huxley's motto: 'Mending is better than ending'.

Climate Chaos: a Unifying Force

Susana: It would be ideal to tax heavily all the dirty industries, but to me, it should be the ethical choice on their part, seeing the situation, seeing the imminent danger the planet is in, seeing the danger we're in. There should be some kind of like moral awakening which makes them stop polluting the planet.

Roc: I think what you're saying is that the problem of evil should be solved. And I would agree with that. Except that, as Kafka said, and I'm sexying him up, evil is what we call the attempt to eradicate evil. He called the final destruction of evil a lunatic dream, by which he thought evil is not weakened but strengthened and accelerated.

Susana: Did he mean evil should be seduced rather than destroyed? Some evil is unseduceble. Faced with evil, indifference and passivity become faces of evil. In a way, we were talking about unifying. I think climate change could be a unifying force that goes beyond right, left or whatever politics. It could be a unifying force.

Roc: It is the ultimate *other*. If you need an other to unite you as a society, often a gender or a race or whatever is used. Make it climate disaster, nature collapse, and then everyone can start working together. So, yes. Perhaps you're saying that we need a spiritual rebirth that would show the people running fossil fuel companies that they can't go on doing it. And the people consuming the fossil fuels, too—the drivers, the people heating their homes with gas. Like even in the fossil fuel companies, many of those people have children and grandchildren and nephews and nieces, and once the children understand, it will be very difficult for those people not to change. So maybe the problem of evil will after all be solved. But I suspect if so, only in this case. Evil will always be with us.

Slavery, Colonialism and Climate Change

Susana: Maybe it'd be like with the abolition of slavery. Something that was unspeakably unethical, and it continued on and on until ...

Roc: Yeah. I often think how horrific it must have been for them. But in Britain at least, it wasn't the people who owned the slaves realising that what they were doing was repulsive and spontaneously releasing them. It took slave rebellions, and slave testimonies and memoirs, and the courts saying there's no such thing as a slave in England. And so, the people who thought they had slaves, the slaves could just walk away. It shows that law can sometimes be a force for good, or at least refrain from being a force for evil. That was in the eighteenth century. And then Parliament followed, partly driven by the Quakers, and at the start of the nineteenth century they banned the international slave trade and blockaded Africa to catch the slave ships, and the Royal Navy started chasing slave traders and releasing the slaves. Then in the 1830s and 40s, they made laws that all the existing slaves should be released all over the British Empire, and the Royal Navy attacked slave-trading places like Brazil and Nigeria.

So, it wasn't the people so-called 'owning' the slaves who realised what they were doing was wrong. It was others getting the government to induce them to stop, using violence if need be. And the same might be true with fossil fuels. I don't think the airlines or motorists or people with gas central heating will spontaneously stop, at least not all of us. We haven't stopped yet—people are still buying fossil cars and gas boilers. We'll have to be stopped by the rest of us. And that's a problem, because most of us are implicated.

Susana: Yes, fossil fuel capitalism is a totalitarian system in that it makes us complicit, in different degrees, with ecocide. The degree of implication, and the blood-stained climate lies, have to be taken into account. Most of us have to become educators, repeating endlessly in endless conversations how lethal gas and oil are until most of us choose to do the least damage. Many people can't afford an eco-friendly boiler or a heat pump, and can't conceive life without their cars, which they can't afford to replace. The transition to clean energy needs to be funded and reimagined. One thing we can all do is to switch to clean energy or at least the least damaging options. There are companies that can't supply clean energy in your area, but all your money goes to the green grid. It goes without saying that progress cannot be part of a colonialist, extractivist and ecocidal project. Going back to slavery, the Abolition Act was explicitly racist. It declared that abolition amounted to expropriation and that slave owners must therefore be compensated for their loss! I recently found out that taxpayers are still paying for the loan that was taken to compensate slave owners. Can you imagine, being the child or grandchild of slaves and discovering that? ... It is essential to publicly shame dirty industries so that they look as unacceptable and hideous as slave traders became. But would that force governments into action? We come back to the oil lobbying problem.

Roc: Well, you've maybe never been in the position where you've had to ransom someone. I have slave relations, allegedly, who that side of my family tried to ransom. They were spotted working as slaves in Algiers after their ship disappeared in the North Sea. The family sent someone to Algiers to buy their freedom, and their 'owner' would have got the money, only they couldn't find them, they'd probably died—up to a half died each year. I've been told there's a memorial to my ancestor and his slave family in the English Church in Algiers. And remember Cervantes—we wouldn't have *Don Quixote*, one of the first and best novels, if he hadn't been ransomed out of slavery. Whatever they paid for him, it was ultra-cheap. Because to me it's Cervantes who was important, even if his 'owner' ended up with filthy cash. Cervantes said liberty and honour were more important than anything else in life, and captivity its greatest evil. As a slave, he should know. But maybe what you are saying is that the British Government shouldn't have paid the ransom needed to get the slaves freed, but should have forced the slave owners to release them instead. That's exactly what happened in North Africa—I think the last European slaves were freed by force in the 1830s. And it's what happened in the American South. I don't know the primary historical detail, so I'm just talking on the basis of shallow insights and would be happy to adjust them to better fit the evidence if corrected. But for me it's more important that the slaves go free, that's the priority, and for the British to be still paying for that—it's the least they could do.

Susana: That's a strong argument. To stop harming human and nonhuman life as soon as possible is vital. It makes enormous sense. At the same time, this solution feels profoundly unfair. It feels like being lied to, poisoned, plunged into catastrophe, killed, and having to compensate the culprit. Climate justice wants to be addressed in the fairest of ways, starting with dirty fossil energy companies. It's interesting you talk about 'ransom', because it places the fossil fuel industry in the context of criminality. We're dealing with racketeering. We are dealing with economic criminals, gangsters, major offenders. You're raising many interesting things at once. Cervantes was extremely lucky, and I wonder how many Cervanteses we've lost through slavery. I love many of Cervantes's works. His stories are so witty, sagacious and contemporary. By the way, *Don Quixote* is one of my favourite novels and the only one that has made me cry. I cried at the end. But going back to slavery, while the lives of others are the most important thing, compensating the oil industry perpetuates injustice and inflicts financial violence on taxpayers. The compensation should have gone to the freed slaves. What happened is shameful and barbaric. Could the British vote on it? Nope. It was a government loan to be paid by British taxpayers so that, although slave ownership pervaded many areas of society, the extraordinarily rich could continue being extraordinarily rich. Feels like a familiar racket to me. Those affected by slavery are still owed reparations. But, yes, at that point, the abolition of slavery demanded swift action.

Roc: Perhaps there are scenarios where it could have been done more quickly by using violence, but I'm not sure. My guess is that if that was a genuine option for the British, they would have taken it, because it was a huge amount of money for them which could have been spent on something else. Look what happened in the American Revolution—the Declaration of Independence cited obliquely, as a grievance, the British emancipation of escaped US slaves. And the US Congress ordered George Washington to retrieve them from the British so as to re-enslave them. It was nearly another century and millions of deaths before the slaves were finally freed in America by using violence. Could have been quicker and cheaper and far better from the point of view of the slaves, who are the ones who matter in this equation, to have so-called 'bought' them and liberated them, as well as for all the people who died in the civil war, and their families—a quarter of the soldiers died—even if it meant the slave owners would have ended up with some filthy cash. It's what I would choose if I was a slave, or a conscript.

Susana: Yes, and anyone who had an ounce of humanity would choose that for the victims too. We have to use all tools available, and each challenge might require a different key. We can learn from the abolition of slavery. When it comes to the end of dirty fossil energy, we can't use it fully as a referent or precedent. And, sadly, modern slavery continues.

Roc: All slavery is horror, which is why eating seafood is so dangerous— it's riddled with moral heavy metals, much of it fished as it is by modern slaves. When people moan about slavery and go on guzzling fish you know they don't really care about slavery, but scoring moral brownie points while indulging it instead. So look at the arguments. Figure what your criterion for the better outcome is—is it utilitarianism, Rawlsianism, some ranked set of human rights. Be morally rational. Try to see through the propaganda embedded in language. Care about the slaves—they're incommensurably more valuable than the slave 'owners;' try not to get diverted by your hatred of mundane evil people from helping those living with violence, fast & slow. Then do something about it. As Nietzsche might say, a great evil is rarely defeated except by allying your cause with some great error. It took belief in an invisible sky god to help dismantle the slavery incumbents. It may take equal degrees of error to destroy the oil & gas community.

Susana: That's quite a statement. To err is human, so mistakes will be made. Do you mean the error being sacrificing climate justice? ... I didn't know about fish and modern slavery. The list of injustices goes on and on. Ultimately, it's about greed and psychopathy. Utter insanity. The right to life, a healthy environment, housing and not being displaced are fundamental. What I'm talking about is normalising a dialogue about financial reparations to the countries impacted by climate breakdown, and apologising. I'm talking about justice and human decency.

Roc: What really is indecent is the government paying to keep dirty sunset industries on ventilators—oil & gas, the airlines, cars etc. In terms of human suffering delivered that completely dwarfs paying them to close down. Best of all though, if you could do it without escalating the violence, would be to recover from the oil & gas companies and the oil & gas sovereign wealth funds like the Norwegian and the Saudi Arabian, a little something towards the immense damage they have caused, above all, since at least the 1970s we now know, in funding climate denial and impeding the transition to renewables. They're still at it. I know we don't blame and shame, but if anything is, that's worthy of a Nuremberg.

Susana: Yes, there's talk about climate genocide. Big Oil is a killing machine. If there was climate justice, they would have to sit at the dock and pay trillions to compensate for the criminal damage they have caused. Of course, the US contributed its fair share in climate denial. As did other countries, including the UK. But it seems you're saying different things—or at least it comes across that way.

Roc: If someone won't do what you want them to do, you can either use violence or persuasion. You may not be strong enough to force them, much as you'd like to, especially if like Saudi Arabia or Russia they used the cash you bought the oil with to stock up on weapons. Russia, and Saudi Arabia have been described as oil companies with armies—but ExxonMobil, Chevron are oil companies with armies too—it's just they don't need their own because the US army and US government are at their disposal. If so, you're going to have to negotiate, and that'll probably involve more cash, just as it did with the slave 'owners.'

Susana: In the meantime, consider not buying any more oil or gas—they'll just persevere in their being.

Roc: Yes, maybe I can make the analogy with rainforest. You can use violence to stop the oil pumping or the rainforest being cut down if you have sufficient military and moral resources at your disposal—but Saudi Arabia and Russia both have powerful and belligerent war machines, and Brazil would snappily accuse you of colonialism—even though it's in self-defence. Or else you can incentivise it in some way—perhaps by enabling renewable investment and generating the undercutting that would already be doing away with much of the emissions if it wasn't for political queering of markets. Every option has to be kept on the table—we may need them all. There are good arguments on all sides—but it makes sense to focus on the outcome for the oppressed—those of us who have died and will die violently from climate and nature collapse—and to optimise that, even if there are accidental side-benefits for the oppressors, because the oppressed are the ones who matter. Otherwise you're violating Kant's precept that people can't be used—you are harming the oppressed to gratify your wish to punish the oppressors. Or even just to signal this. Unless it's done *pour encourager les autres*, because there is moral hazard from the slave 'owners' thinking they will be compensated, so they buy more slaves, and that's a really strong argument. We are seeing something similar now, with airline bailouts and bank bailouts. I am sure the oil companies, with their stranded wells and refineries and obscene decommissioning costs which they are counting on us covering for them, will pay out all they can in dividends and bonuses and then join the bleating queue for bailouts, and are even buying soon-to-be-stranded assets, counting on a pay-out. It's politics, it's disgusting, but not as disgusting as missing any opportunity to stop the oil gushing.

Susana: Of course, time is of the essence when it comes to saving lives and mitigating climate and biodiversity collapse. And yes, I certainly mean to discourage further bailouts. Remember? During the global financial crisis, when banks collapsed, Iceland jailed its bankers rather than bailed them out ... Let's foreground corruption and massively protest against specific laws that protect dirty business, and what Joseph Stiglitz, the Nobel Prize-winning economist, recently called 'litigation terrorism.' Obviously, we urgently need new laws, policies, rules and business ethics. System change is vital. The geopolitical order has to change. The fossil fuels industry is out of order. The dirty fossil energy orgy is over. The moral outrage has to keep on growing. What are climate breakdown and biodiversity destruction about? They're about greed. And colonising the atmosphere. And racism, human exceptionalism and mass murder. The omnicide lobby has to be stopped. How can the perpetrators of the greatest crime against all life on earth not be prosecuted? Of course, there is a relationship between colonialism, extreme weather, and the Global South. The colonial mindset is still there.

Roc: Yes, and also the way anyone still using fossil fuels is colonising the future. Almost everyone in the world now is part of the world historical 1% in terms of the resources we are splurging and the harm we are doing, compared with those who came before and those, if any, who will come after us. Some far more than others, obviously—some of us, the private jet set, the CEOs, are mass murderers on an operatic scale, but even the most modest who fill their moped with gas are serial killers, enabling the business model of the mass murder folk. It is very hard not to be complicit when the invitations are so subtle, so nearly irresistible, and so everywhere. Especially if you are desperate. We are living in a world where it is not possible to be clean. But we have to learn how to decline these invitations—we are moralising with beams in our eyes, to use the language of the Bible. It makes me think of Blanqui—'A noisy humanity infatuated with its own grandeur, believing itself to be the universe and living in its prison as though in some immense realm, only to founder at an early date along with its globe, which has borne with deepest disdain the burden of human arrogance.' And we—hiya!

Savannah: Sorry, I just went in the kitchen and your ratatouille wasn't doing so well.

Roc: Oh, did you turn it off?

Savannah: I turned it off but it's not looking—

Roc: Is it burnt?

Savannah: It's quite burnt. Sad, crispy.

Roc: Oh no!

Savannah: I just thought I'd let you know.

Roc: Thank you my darling, will you shut the door?

Savannah: Yes of course.

Roc: Thanks.

Waterloo Bridge: It Was Very, Very Wonderful

An honest deed is sweetened by its cost. *Lucan.*

In surrendering our mass storytelling function to entities whose first priority is profit, we make a dangerous concession: 'Tell us', we say in effect, 'as much truth as you can, while still making money'. This is not the same as asking: 'Tell us the truth'. *George Saunders*

Non-Violent Direct Action

Susana: When I first started following XR on Twitter, I was dazzled by this amazing organism, this unfolding intelligence, but it was only when I watched Roger Hallam's videos that I could complete the puzzle. Looking at his work, would you agree that his approach has worked? It's such a powerful mix of tactics.

Roc: Yes. It's an understatement to say XR is not just Roger, but his focus on non-violent direct action …

Susana: It drew me in, yeah.

Roc: Only, back then, at my first contact, it wasn't called XR.

Susana: Did it have a name?

Roc: It had names which weren't as good as Extinction Rebellion. I suppose it was called Rising Up or Compassionate Revolution or Stop Killing Londoners. It came from a long global tradition of resistance.

Susana: Did you do things with Rising Up?

Roc: Not so much. I agreed mostly with XR, but I could see some things with Rising Up which I didn't completely agree with. What happens to me often is I agree about what the problem is, most good-willed people do, if they are willing to think with any rigour, but I don't necessarily agree over what the solution is, because I'm very evidence-based. It's not because I want different solutions, but because I have a different idea of the mechanisms which connect the different resources and components of a system. In fact I find many people almost wholly unrealistic in their thinking about solutions, perhaps above all in failing to acknowledge any natural constraints or trade-offs at all. Some people's line—perhaps the mainstream line at present—is you can have whatever you want in a society and all constraints are imaginary. I don't think that's true. Their response to that is there's no such thing as truth. And we can't usually get beyond that.

It's maybe the same thing as I was saying about taking the empirical approach towards what works in environmental protest itself. I like looking at the world, seeing what's worked before, what hasn't. And doing experiments, seeing what emerges. I find a lot of organisations don't do that. They take an emotive approach or an ideological approach or a rationalist approach or an inertial approach or whatever, but it often seems to me that what they're doing is going to make the problem worse, because they haven't understood the mechanisms creating the problem. So often I will agree with a group like Rising Up about what the problem is—it's usually easy to identify—and even what the method to address it is, like NVDA, but I won't agree about the much harder question of what the nuts and bolts of the solution is, and then it's difficult to fully join the group.

Evil fights Back

Roc: W. H. Auden said the trouble with fighting evil is evil fights back, and it generates more evil. And there's no time to create beauty. Unless it's non-violent, really all you're doing is adding to the problem because you're adding to the stock of evil in the world. And so, in a way, the only way to fight evil is non-violent. Even if you lose, at least you were in the right! But anyway, there are many times when evil has been fought violently, and it had to be fought violently. But, so I take it back. It's not true.

Susana: Violence can't be completely avoided. Non-violence is a better way of dealing with conflict. All studies on psychology and social movements say so.

Roc: And non-violence may be more powerful, so it's expedient as well as moral and beautiful.

Susana: I don't like the idea of solving a conflict through violence, if there are better ways.

Roc: Yes. But I'm thinking about say the Spanish Civil War or the Second World War, and maybe it's naive and entitled to imagine one could have solved those problems with non-violence. I don't know. Not even violence solved them. In the Second World War, the approach of many of the Jewish and other people sent to the death camps was non-violent, and that didn't solve much. But maybe they didn't want to be forced into complicity by being violent themselves, and that must be honoured.

Susana: Something that I would like to research—I have, a bit—is what makes peaceful societies work. Sometimes, it's partly to do with language and interesting taboos. They're very small societies and that allows them to work better. War and warfare commerce are, of course, inconceivable. War is business. Of course, with bigger societies ... In Britain ...

Roc: I think in Britain, because we have *relatively* benign police and a *relatively* benign criminal justice system, compared to other places in the world which make your hair stand on end, we're all privileged relative to other places and we have a duty to use that privilege to get this change to happen. Because it's much harder for people in other places with much more ruthless systems to actually do what we're doing here. And often they are still trying, even so, and paying with their lives. We are fortunate here, so far. That could change, it could all flip into the torture and disappearance and football stadium scenario that's happening elsewhere. I've been looking at footage of Moscow and Hong Hong. It makes me cry. Even Paris—the way the police sprayed pepper gas into XR people's eyes at close range, who were just sitting there in a protest. It can really change, and we have to be ready for that.

Declaration of Climate Emergency

Susana: And yet, despite all the NVDA, nothing has happened here in Britain apart from a Climate Emergency being declared. That day I was there, in Parliament Square. It was packed. I was with my brother and mother, who, as you know were part of the Rebellion from the beginning, my mother's wheelchair always carrying the XR flag high. Caroline Lucas, Farhana Yamin, Ash Sarkar and others gave speeches. We were waiting to hear from Parliament. And then, Jeremy Corbyn, who had called the motion, came and announced a national declaration of an Environment and Climate Emergency. Everyone was ecstatic. After the declaration, we did the Carnival of Chaos, we banged pots and pans at the Brazilian Embassy to protest Bolsonaro's destruction of the Amazon. That was May Day. What day is it today? I mean no action whatsoever has come forth, the expansion of airports is still on the menu?

Roc: I think two big things have happened. One is, the mass media have changed the way they are talking about the climate disaster and ecological collapse. And there are some very terrible statistics. I can remember two, I think. One is that ... Well, I might garble them a bit, and maybe they are fake news. One was that I think in 2017 the big US networks combined had a total of two hours coverage of climate change for the whole year. And those two hours were almost all reporting of President Trump coming out of the Paris Climate Accord. And then another statistic, for Britain, I can't remember which year exactly, but it was fairly recently, that there still was more coverage of a child who was kidnapped maybe ten or twelve years ago than, amongst other things, all the children who are dying now. There was still more coverage of her in the UK media than there was of climate collapse or even the whole of the environment. Even though, by focusing on her and not covering the climate and biodiversity emergencies, they are sacrificing countless other children. And what XR delivered, together with all the other people working on this—is more honest reporting of the environmental disaster. What it failed to deliver, however, was honest reporting about what has to be done about it for anything to change.

Susana: I absolutely agree, there is now a huge change in public awareness. Since the Rebellion, I noticed an increase in stories about climate breakdown on my social media newsfeed ... But yes, the youth strikes, Fridays for Future, are great. Greta Thunberg is a godsend. She's brilliant!

Roc: So, the youth strikes, and David Attenborough's film. But I think David Attenborough might have been slightly provoked into action by XR and the environmental movement, because I seem to remember there was a certain amount of us saying to David Attenborough, before he came out, 'How can you be making people imagine that there isn't this immense disaster happening?'

Susana: He was censored by the BBC. He couldn't really speak about environmental problems. And when he did 'Our Planet' with Netflix, Netflix took a different approach, which was to acknowledge ecological collapse and climate change. It seems that the BBC had deliberately missed the boat to engage in ecological issues with Attenborough's documentaries. Netflix didn't. But Attenborough knows very well what's happening, and he's been persuasive through showing us the beauty of our planet. And that has been beautifully effective. He's been persuasive through showing us our plastic planet, the plastic tsunami ravaging the environment. That had an enormous impact on people. But for many years he couldn't really articulate what was happening with global warming and many species, because he was censored.

Roc: He may have been censored in the BBC, and the BBC is operating a sort of censorship racket. And, for instance, I was very amused. We had an XR action outside the BBC. I'm not sure whether you were there, but XR put them into lockdown. Towards the end of 2018, I think it was. In London, and one or two regional offices of the BBC too.

Susana: There is a recurrent problem with the BBC not reporting on climate change. They didn't report anything.

Roc: And they didn't report being put in lockdown by XR! And to me that sums up the whole thing of the BBC. There's a statue of George Orwell outside the BBC which again is hilarious in a way, because they are Orwell's Ministry of Truth. So Attenborough, he may have been censored by the BBC but that wouldn't have stopped him saying: 'Enough! I can't be censored anymore. I'm going to different outlets.' It would have been hard to censor that news. But I agree it's a problem and the fact that he has now overcome the censorship, fantastic! I think XR, I mean it's explicitly part of our policy to move the Overton window, which means the kind of things you're allowed to talk about in public discourse. And that window moves, and XR explicitly had the aim of moving it so that you were allowed to talk about ecological collapse and climate disaster.

Susana: So that's Tell the Truth, one of the three demands.

Roc: Yeah. So, XR has three goals, as we know. Getting the government to tell the truth which you could say is on its way to being realised. Parliament declaring the Climate Emergency is something. But we also want the government to act as if it was true. And again, they've made a vanishingly inadequate but symbolically significant start which I hope is the thin end of the wedge, with the commitment to be carbon neutral by 2050. XR's second goal is to become net zero in greenhouse gas emissions by 2025. Which is shorthand for having a reasonable chance of hitting 1.5° rise in temperature—already far too lethal in my view—but a valid milestone on the way to climate repair. And the third goal is to convene a Citizens' Assembly, which is like a sort of jury blown up to maybe a thousand people representing all the different parts of the population to listen to experts and then decide on policies to achieve this.

What do you feel about those other goals? I mean I suspect both of us are completely behind telling the truth and acting as if it was true as a goal of XR.

Susana: I wish they were achieved. I wish they were possible, and I think they are. We're in 2019. It's a very short time. When I first saw the demand of zero carbon emissions by 2025, I thought it was trying to push the government to act, and it wasn't a realistic demand. It was deliberately aiming too high. But the more I read, the more I realised it is the action urgently needed to keep the world below catastrophic sea levels, to stop climate change damaging the environment further, in an irreversible way, and prevent ecological collapse. But just six years to get rid of cars? To get rid of aviation? How can that happen? How can that happen when there's so many vested interests at stake, when we don't have alternatives in place? We don't have alternatives for traveling abroad ... Well, we have trains, but trains should be made much cheaper, as cheap as flights. The countryside tends to have a poor public transport system, so we need investment in public transport infrastructure. We have a very multicultural society, which takes flights often, and people with disabilities who need cars, and some of us need cars to visit our elderly, ailing relatives. We need trucks and lorries to transport things. So how to bring about that change?

Roc: It is very difficult. But not as difficult as staying alive, if we don't do it, will be.

Susana: One thing that is vital is to halt the fossil fuel industry in the way it's going. It's vital to keep fossil fuels in the ground. To stop all the companies that are damaging the planet in manifold ways from damaging it further. That would be the most urgent thing to do.

Roc: You mean stop them growing or you mean close them down?

Susana: Certainly stop them growing, yes. Completely and utterly. Yes. A complete conversion to renewables. Apparently, the renewable industry is not ready to take on so many people. If everyone wanted to convert to green energy, it wouldn't be possible because it hasn't grown fast enough to do that. So, yes, we need a rapid transition. The government has to provide home insulation on a large scale. And we need a huge investment to make non-damaging or less damaging alternatives affordable to everyone. Solar panels are so expensive, let alone wind turbines. And renters, a large proportion of people in the UK, aren't able to have them installed. So, this is a huge problem. The government has to step in. And if it doesn't, we have to keep on protesting, boycotting harmful activities and delegitimising the powers that be.

Plato's Guardians

Roc: I do wonder whether the Citizens' Assembly will come up with the decisions that XR thinks, because if you look at, say, the voting recently—

Susana: That is a fear of mine.

Roc: Yeah, so I wouldn't rely entirely on a Citizens' Assembly. I think it's brilliant to add it to the mix, but I'm not convinced it will come up with the policies we need, unfortunately. I believe in power being divided up. I don't like it when power gets centralised. So, if there is a Citizens' Assembly to represent the people, as well as a House of Commons, a House of Lords, a monarch, and a legal system, and academia, and the media, and theatre, and cinema, and all the other places where there's chunks of power, the more the better, providing they're non-aligned.

Susana: The Citizens' Assembly will be informed by a body of independent scientists, plus a body of independent specialists who know how to solve the problems that we have, how to reach the targets that we have, and who are independent, not bought by corporations. Somehow, they cannot be appointed by the government, they have to be truthful, and they have to be honest.

Roc: But experts can be corrupted, and many 'experts' are corrupt, and the whole concept of expert is discredited in a way, because to corrupt the experts is the first gambit of industry and finance, if they don't like what the experts might otherwise say. Plato's solution was to have 'Guardians,' who were physically fit, polyamorous mathematicians. You put guardians in charge of the society, and the guardians aren't allowed to own anything. So, Plato wanted to make it hard for them to be corrupted by saying the guardians have to live in, like, a communistic way where they can't have possessions. And they are the ones who take the decisions for the society. And they can't be corrupted, because you can't buy them, because if you give them money, they aren't allowed to have it. So that's one solution. It's the reverse of the traditional communist setup, where the elite have all the possessions and the people live without property rights.

But I do have misgivings. I think it'll be a massive net benefit to have a Citizens' Assembly, as well as other structures, but I have misgivings about whether a Citizens' Assembly will actually deliver the right answers. I think they might want more cars, and more planes, and more consumerism. It's the carnival of things, what in the 'Money Kindergarten' section of *Philosophical Toys* you've called the mesmerising power of fetishism, a collective ritualised excess. And it's not even that getting what you want actually makes you feel better, it's just that it releases you from the pain of wanting it. And on the 2025 aim, it's ambitious, but we need ambition. And I do think it's doable, myself, but obviously I'm not sure it will be done.

Susana: Plato's Guardians idea is brilliant! I wonder why it hasn't taken off?

It was Very, Very Wonderful

Roc: Susana, I wanted to ask you about what happened to you during the Easter Rebellion. Because I think that's interesting.

Susana: Do you want to answer that question first?

Roc: What, me? What happened to me?

Susana: Yeah!

Roc: Okay. Lots of different things happened, maybe it's hard to talk about, but lots of different things happened to me. And I had some amazing times! The ones that spring to mind are on Parliament Square. Two nights in a row the police overcame Parliament Square. The first night we were down to about six people lying in the road, and hundreds of police people, it seemed like hundreds and hundreds. And we were finished. And suddenly more people started coming and there were seven people and eight people and nine people and ten people. It was amazing. And then there was the sound of the samba band, this incredibly loud drumming. Unbelievable, that shook your body inside your ribs and vibrated your brain inside your skull. And the samba arrived which was maybe a hundred people and maybe there were another hundred people with them and just the force of the noise and the rhythm and the band just swept away the police as if they were like nothing. Rhythm trumped force. And the square was taken back by XR. It was so moving!

I was worried just for a moment because the momentum with which the samba band arrived and swept away the police didn't stop there, and the samba overshot and went out onto Westminster Bridge. And I could see that they might suck back the police in their wake, back into the square. And it was beginning to happen. So, I was worried that we would lose it again, but actually then the band washed back, just in time.

So that was the first night which I think was the Wednesday night, and then on the Thursday night the same thing happened but with even more police. So many police that I just didn't think there *were* so many police. It was like there was hardly any space for all the police to be. Because they were just packed in like hi-viz sardines. They could hardly move, there were so many of them. And again, they came back into the square and started taking people away and taking down the barricades and I'll tell you what happened, it's interesting. I'd been on Parliament Square earlier in the day and the Rebel Rider cyclists went by and I didn't have any particular role then on Parliament Square, and nothing was happening there, it was all quiet, so I just got on my bicycle and went with the Rebel Riders.

Susana: When was that?

Roc: That was on Thursday evening I think, on the first Thursday of the Easter Rebellion. So, I went with them and we went past Buckingham Palace. As we passed the palace and my neighbouring cyclist gestured angrily at it, I started setting out the hidden purpose of a constitutional monarchy—which is to have that dangerous role of head of state already occupied by an un-legitimated nonentity, and therefore unavailable to a Trump or a Maduro. However, my neighbour cycled off looking alarmed and cross before I could finish. And we ended up outside the BBC. But then I got a message over my comms saying Parliament Square was under attack by the police. So, I immediately started shouting to the Rebel Rider cyclists at the BBC, 'Quick, quick, come to Parliament Square because we need help.' But they were making so much noise that nobody could hear me, and I was making gestures which they couldn't understand. Everyone was making gestures, so I couldn't get myself noticed. So, in the end I left them at the BBC and went alone to Parliament Square, feeling thwarted and beaten. But on the way, to my joy, I saw the samba band at Piccadilly Circus. And again, I tried to get them to come to Parliament Square. 'Quick, quick, come to Parliament Square, we're going to lose it!' But they were making so much noise that again they couldn't hear me, and couldn't understand the gestures I was making. So again, the same thing happened, and I went to Parliament Square and I've just never seen so many police, it was completely unbelievable. And they were taking everyone—

Susana: Were you fearful, were you feeling anxious?

Roc: I got in a very interesting state of almost jubilation and a sort of primate thing came over me where I was behaving very like a monkey, like I had my arms up and I was making a lot of whooping and chattering noises and I was dancing around sideways on two bent legs, my knees opened wide, like monkeys do. It was almost like my feet were hands. But all the same, the square was gonna fall. It was falling.

Susana: Parliament Square, I was there at some point when you needed to be there, so I went, and it was like not that many people, and the samba band came in to energise us. So, hope was always in the air. I was always trying to share messages from Twitter, Facebook, telling rebels where they were needed. But there weren't that many police when I was there, so your experience is more like: 'This is really critical!'

Roc: It varied a lot, the police, yeah. So again, we were down to the last few people on Parliament Square when the Rebel Rider cyclists came at last, and the cyclists started circling round the square and making it very hard for the police to operate because there were all these bicycles going by. Round and round, like a mesmerising wheel. But it wasn't enough. I was going so fast in my chimp state that the police in their *gilets jaunes* were unable to stop me and to me they turned into this kind of dayglo mist. 'Can't catch me,' or so I thought. And sure enough, eventually one of them grabbed me as I went past. So, I just talked to the police person for an ultra-long time and made the conversation really captivating, the idea being to get him completely distracted so he would forget to arrest not only me, but anyone else. It's all on film on his chest-mounted video camera and I'd love to see that. But in the end, after rather an involved and interesting conversation, he suddenly came to himself with some kind of effort of will, and said I had to go away from the square or be locked up right now and I didn't want to be locked up right now so I went away from the square. But then just as I went away, heading back to Waterloo Bridge where I really belonged, I heard the thudding sound of drumming! So I knew the samba band had come, and hoped that the same thing would happen as the night before. That again it would be saved from the police. So I tried to come back in, but couldn't find a way past the police. But it was saved! So that was two amazing nights on Parliament Square. Tell me your most amazing experiences.

Susana: I'd say it was the overall experience. The Rebellion embodied the crystallisation of a new type of consciousness I thought would mark the new millennium. I knew it was there. But it was only during the Rebellion that I saw it crystallised. On Waterloo Bridge, I had a glimpse of Utopia. The energy was extraordinary. I loved the trees we took there, the plants, the flowers, life, and I loved seeing the bold and colourful variety of XR flags, some with bees, butterflies, hearts, skulls, waving high in the air. In the future, there will be a blue plaque at Waterloo Bridge commemorating the Rebellion. It was there that I really felt that there was a kind of high form of collective intelligence taking over. I felt that very strongly there, being part of all those beautiful and empathetic people sharing and cooperating with everything. There were rebels from all over the UK. The loveliest people, all gathered in one point in space. We all felt truly useful. It was a profound shared experience ... The well-being area was such a clever idea, and it was heartening that the church had opened its doors to us, so we could store things there, or just chill out. It was so hot, and 'Ecocide Man' was there every day, dressed as an owl, holding his Stop Ecocide placards. I really admired his staying power. He must have been unbearably hot in his owl costume. It was also great the evening the stage-truck was surrounded by police, and we were messaging late at night. From my end, it all seemed lost, and you were there, liaising with the police, and assured me we'd be there the following day, and then, amazingly, the bridge wasn't taken that night. I felt truly elated coming back to the bridge in the morning. It was a journey from intense fear to an all-pervasive winning feeling. It was also the most crowded and jubilant day.

Also, I was pleased to start the Rebellion as a writer, by reading at different XR sites. I felt honoured to read 'Dear Angelus Novus' in the extravagant but relevant TELL THE TRUTH pink boat, which blocked the traffic in Oxford Circus for over a week. I felt honoured to be part of a historic event. The TELL THE TRUTH boat was dedicated to Berta Cáceres, the environmental activist from Honduras, who was assassinated. It is a homage to her, as well as to all those who have been killed as a result of defending their land, telling the truth about corporate polluters. So, I was very conscious of that. And I went to Oxford Circus twice because you needed to be there. And the energy there was also extraordinary, with all these lovely people dancing, and everyone was so kind and gentle. I went to all the sites. Every day, I tried to keep in touch with what was happening on all the sites.

Roc: They were very different, the sites. It was interesting what a different energy each site had.

Susana: Like Waterloo Bridge, Oxford Circus was delightfully chaotic, and Marble Arch was a kind of more peaceful and calmer site, but they had a piano with the speakers run by rebels on bicycles, so that was quite special. I think Parliament Square, somehow, was not so crowded.

Roc: Except with police.

Susana: I went there twice … And I think it's because everyone was somewhere else, and unlike Waterloo Bridge, Oxford Circus and Piccadilly Circus, it was a site which didn't block the traffic permanently. I really enjoyed the play about fossil fuels on Waterloo Bridge. I think you were locked-on under the stage-truck.

Roc: Yes, I got the sound but not the sight because it was taking place while I was locked to the drive shaft. And it sounded lovely, it sounded wonderful. Yeah. When there were bands on the stage truck, stomping out time just by my head, and I couldn't block my ears because my hands were padlocked, that was tricky. But otherwise, it was really serene—the calm eye of a furious moral storm.

Susana: There was a kind of egoless atmosphere. The atmosphere, sheer cooperation, it was lovely.

Roc: It's interesting, but I wonder whether … It's a bit like the story of the three little pigs and the wolf, in that the police were trying to blow it all down, day after day after day. Huffing and puffing. I wonder whether that made it … Definitely added to the atmosphere of it in a strange way. It wouldn't have been the same without the police trying to take us away. And it possibly made it more beautiful, it's interesting. And more symbolical, there was a sort of symbolism to the fact that this joy was happening on little islands being battered by waves of police.

Susana: Yeah, you could be arrested any time. It could end any time …

Roc: Like life itself.

Susana: There was also this pervasive feeling of hope. Many things were going right with the Rebellion, and we were there day after day. I suppose most of us experienced similar feelings of celebration, joy, hope, pride at what we were doing. These feelings I've had from the beginning with XR's imaginative actions, and whenever I saw them covered in the media. It was so exhilarating being there, we felt the Rebellion was a success, there was this elation at overcoming the odds, but we were always dealing with this edge of tension, the presence of the police, and the fact that you could be arrested at any moment. Whenever anyone was arrested, we would all clap and chant: 'WE LOVE YOU'. We would chant 'We love you', but you know, it was mixed emotions, really. Someone is being dragged, they're going to be in a cell for you don't know how long, maybe pay a fine. So, on the one hand the idea was to get as many people as possible arrested, at the same time you feel ... Do you have to get arrested to make a point about something all scientists agree on ... You know, completely mixed emotions about the arrests. It's good for grabbing the headlines, but then it saddens and angers me. Unfortunately I can't be arrested because I'm caring for my mum, and there must be many rebels in the same situation. I found it really beautiful seeing grandfathers and grandmothers there, begging to be arrested, and doing it for everyone, for their grandchildren. I found that really moving.

Roc: There's a novella by Wells, *The Time Machine*, where there's a society where people are very innocent and they're picnicking and playing and making music, but at night these creatures come up from underground and take them away.

Susana: The Morlocks!

Roc: Yeah. And it's a little like that.

Susana: The Morlocks were right there in front of you!

Roc: Yeah, they come in the daytime now, the Morlocks, in police vans. They don't wait till night.

Susana: So many Morlocks! But the Morlocks are supposed to be the working class in 'The Time Machine'.

Roc: I think Wells is talking about the future of the working class.

Susana: That is still, you know, oppressed. The day before Waterloo Bridge was taken, it was cordoned off at the south end. There were vast amounts of police and police vans, and I couldn't get to the bridge, so I had interesting conversations with the police about the necessity of doing what we were doing, and about climate change. I realised many of them were saying they're overworked, they don't have time to find out about climate change. So I said, just google it. Just find out about it. I told them some people say the real threat are the youth strikes, not XR. They didn't know about Greta Thunberg or the youth strikes. But there was eagerness to learn about things, some police people gathered around me and listened, and I found that heartening.

Roc: I'm sure there's a lot of very different views within the police. For instance, there was a time where I was on Parliament Square, negotiating with the police, and the Silver, the police officer in charge of trying to take it back from us, he looked into my eyes and said: 'I don't agree with everything you're doing, but I agree with almost everything.'

Susana: Good.

Roc: And I could see in his eyes that he meant it, you know, you can see in someone's eyes when they're telling the truth. It felt like we were both close to tears. But then there's other police who were sarky and nasty and then, at worst the police would lose their tempers and be violent. But not very often. I think it's good how relatively rarely that happened, even compared to somewhere like France. Though it would be amazing if it had been not at all, and that's what we mustn't cease to expect.

Susana: Yes, with the police, you could plainly see that some agreed with what we were doing. And, it was beautiful, especially during the Easter weekend, to see so many families with their children and everyone was having a wonderful time. And I said to a policeman 'Would you like your children to be here?' And he became really serious and said: 'I would never allow my children to go to a protest.' I said to them, 'This is like being in a festival. Are you enjoying yourselves?' And one of them was like 'Yes' and another one was like 'No, I'm just doing my duty, I'm just working.' And he was the one who said he would never allow his children to go to any protest—

Roc: Two police people got in trouble because they danced.

Susana: Yeah, that was wonderful.

Roc: They got in trouble in the press, I don't know whether they got in trouble with the police themselves.

Susana: I saw videos and that was quite wonderful. Because you could see there was a party atmosphere and the policemen were really relaxed.

You could see it was like being in a festival except for wearing the uniform. When I was talking to the police on the bridge, I said: 'Our uniform is nicer, why don't you just take yours off?' Because ... Yeah. Why wear it? I don't know.

Roc: We've spoken about the enriching side of it—but there is obviously a traumatic side, a hurtful side. For me a lot of it's about fear for my children, and stress—not knowing where they are in all the muddle and uproar. I think of the little girl getting lost in *Dr Zhivago*, of the famous pram on the steps in Eisenstein or the runaway pram in *Babar*. It's like those dreams when you have lost your children, but can't speak and can't use your limbs. Also you are going on for more than a week without much food, sleep, toilets, washing, getting dry when you need these. There is noise—drumming and sirens and chanting. The clatter is like what it must have been in a weaving mill—maybe still is if weaving is still done like that. There are more trivial things which bug you. If you leave a good bike locked up in the same place for too long in London it will be liberated. Too long is anything from ten minutes upwards. I love my bike as much as you can love anything inanimate—it's an old Mercian probably from the sixties or seventies—each Mercian has a number so I could look it up. While I was locked to the drive shaft of the truck blocking Waterloo bridge it was as if I had become my bike which was locked in turn to a railing at the end of the bridge. Both of us were waiting for our locks to be sawn or broken and for us to be put in a van and carried away to some lockup full of stolen bikes or some custody centre full of stolen rebels. There is physical exhaustion—I don't know how many miles I was doing on that bike—maybe thirty miles or so at most each day—but often through grid-locked and angry streets whose air is poison, to get to the temporary Edens walled with police. There is continually expecting your home to be raided, potentially to loose your manuscripts, your address book, your emails, access to the records you need to do your VAT, to run your business or do your job, your telephone, your computer. And all this added to the background stress of knowing what is happening to the climate, to countless people all over the world being burned or flooded or displaced or abused by climate conflict, of how much worse it's going to get. And on the other hand, it's an offer you can't refuse—an offer to have courage, at least until things turn really mean, too mean even for that. 'From a real antagonist boundless courage flows into you,' claims Kafka.

Propaganda Model

Susana: So what would you say are XR achievements, so far?

Roc: Chomsky has this propaganda model of the media which is not about truth, it's about propaganda and about conditioning people to behave how you want them to. I think the media has worked very effectively at doing that. And XR has succeeded in breaking that system, at least for now, and I'm sure that system will snap back to being propaganda very quickly, and there's still mostly propaganda in it. But XR showed that you could pierce that system and make the mass media report on climate apocalypse and nature collapse.

So that's one of the achievements. And the other achievement is as we have said, getting the UK Parliament to declare the Climate Emergency. And that is just words, and parliament is full of words, but they're quite powerful words. They actually are powerful, and Parliament as a whole didn't want to say that. It's the last thing it wanted to say, so I think it's an incredible achievement to get Parliament to tell the truth about something it didn't want to tell the truth about. And that just shows the power of XR's non-violent direct action methods.

Susana: It's been fantastic news XR and the Climate Youth Strike. To see them together makes the demands so much stronger, though it was only front-page news on a couple of newspapers, or maybe just one? The BBC barely covered the news, when, of course, it should have been the main news item. It's all about Brexit ... On Channel 4, or maybe on their Twitter account, Jon Snow said Brexit is a drop in the ocean when compared with the existential threat of climate change.

The End is Nigh

Roc: Do you have criticisms of XR?

Susana: Let me think. I haven't thought about that. I think when I first followed XR's account and saw mention of the sixth mass extinction in the brief description, I didn't know what it was. There was so much I didn't know about! To begin with the term sounded apocalyptic. Nostradamus or something. The term is scientifically accurate. But I would have made the description simpler, because generally XR is very accessible, and it welcomes everyone, and I think the three demands are clear. When I was leafletting in the tube, and engaging in conversation with commuters, I realised some terms might not be clear to a lot of people. Again, when you talk about ecological collapse and the sixth extinction, for someone who's new to the subject ... you might sound like a Jehovah's Witness saying the end of the world is nigh ... which it is, unless we act swiftly. Maybe the brief description on Twitter has changed since I last saw it.

Roc: It's the problem of how, well, first the problem of how you know about reality. Like how do we know it's the sixth mass extinction? It's the problem of epistemology, of science in effect. And of cutting through the propaganda simulating science.

And then it's the problem of how you convince someone, the problem of psychology and literature. Once science has told you there is a sixth mass extinction, which it has, how do you then convince other people who don't want to know? Or maybe, how do you explain it to the people who do want to know, and how do you penetrate through to the people who are in denial? It's a big problem.

There is a standard XR talk. Have you heard that? That is for people who haven't heard about XR and they come, and they listen. And that does explain the things you're talking about, and there are slides and there are references to scientific papers. Organisations can say, 'Will you come and give the talk?' I went and gave it right at the beginning, together with Frieda & Roger, after which they came to live with me for a bit. And it's a very upsetting talk, because one is hearing the truth. So it generates a lot of grief and fear, 'oh no, what have we done!', but you have to go through that stage, if you're going to help solve the problem, you have to open your eyes to what's being done.

Susana: You gave that talk, is it online?

Roc: I think it's online in the XR documents. It's evolved since. It's been evolving all the time and being improved. But my experience of XR is, I'm amazed at the achievements and the success. And beauty. I think the success, particularly of the International Rebellion in April, was just incredible.

New Reality Calls for New Stories

Susana: How would you extend the awareness project? Although there's now a lot of awareness, a lot of people don't know what to do about it, there is apathy, or magical thinking. Not wanting to know, as well … How would you educate people into the necessity of taking action? Of mobilising? Maybe culture, maybe making the media tell the truth, which XR is very good at. Education in schools, making sure the schools are teaching climate change, which they've tried not to, trying to improve the education because scientific education is very poor in Britain. The teachers are trying hard, but the outcome in other countries is better.

Roc: Well, I think art, literature, music are important. If music is so powerful and if people love the Rolling Stones or Taylor Swift or whoever, they have incredible power. Writers have incredible power. Actors have incredible power. So—that's one way. People are celebrity-obsessed and if celebrities can be brought over, people will start following their celebrities. Change can happen in societies really fast.

Susana: Yes, of course. There are some amazing eco-warrior celebrities, like Jane Fonda, Leonardo di Caprio, Harrison Ford. In the UK, Emma Thompson backed up the Rebellion, and Massive Attack played in Marble Arch. But what's happening with the rest of British celebrities? And what's happening with the literary world, it's as if we weren't living in a new reality? Or maybe writers who are writing about climate change aren't that visible? Recently, I discovered an amazing large-scale work by Joseph Beuys, an ecological intervention: in the early 80s, he proposed a plan to plant 7000 oak trees throughout Kassel, each paired with a basalt stone, for Documenta 7. With the help of volunteers, he planted them over several years, completely transforming Kassel's cityscape. Isn't it marvellous? The power that art can yield, well, that goes back to the bit of Auden you mentioned, that fighting evil generates evil, and there is no time to create beauty. Beauty is something XR does well! … The Red Brigade—also called The Invisible Circus—with its beautiful red robes and mournful faces is so moving … A moment I really loved after the Rebellion was when I went on an exhilarating XR bike swarm, we were all carrying the Beyond Politics bee flags, and cycled past Somerset House, and there was this fantastic artwork by Justin Brice Guariglia on a large solar-powered LED sign, which reads: WE ARE THE ASTEROID, and, on seeing it, everything fitted to perfection. We need powerful images that translate our predicament. We need good art. We need to act, while creating beauty ... On that high note, I have to leave you—I'm late for Derek. Let's carry on by email.

July 2019 Emails: Codename Project Mushroom

> Hope is not a lottery ticket you can sit on the sofa and clutch, feeling lucky. It is an axe you break down doors with in an emergency. Hope should shove you out the door, because it will take everything you have to steer the future away from endless war, from the annihilation of the earth's treasures and the grinding down of the poor and marginal ... To hope is to give yourself to the future–and that commitment to the future is what makes the present inhabitable. *Rebecca Solnit*

On Saturday, 6 July August 2019, at 09:16, susanamedina@xr.earth wrote:

Dear Iceberg Babushka

Good to see you at the Galley Beggar Press event ...

Wishing you a splendiferous XR Youth Pride—such a great idea to go as an iceberg! x

On Saturday, 6 July 2019, at 12:52, rocsandford@xr.earth wrote:

Thank you, Susana! Hoping I don't melt too soon!

Pity you can't come along. You must feel so tired after your trip! x

On Wednesday, 10 July 2019, at 11:16, susanamedina@xr.earth wrote:

Dear Fabulosa Iceberg Diva,

You did melt!!! XR Youth ... and your children, so lucky to have you!

Thank you for your endeavours ... I just watched the XR Youth Pride video on FB. The evening green dress is beautiful, you're so lucky to walk the pink carpet! It all looks so glam ... but, yes, sad reality.

I have a similar evening green dress ... We could wear them together :) ...

Maybe next time we meet? :) You have to tell me about your last days ... did you know you'd be performing? And what about the police?

Here, some progress with editing my novel.

And so, when are we going to meet next? Missing your stories. Sx

On Wednesday, 10 July 2019, at 11:50, rocsandford@xr.earth wrote:

Hey Susana—really glad you like the melting iceberg!—yes would love to go out with you, both in our green dresses. Perhaps the melting iceberg needs a fellow lady-berg x

On Wednesday, 10 July 2019, at 13:37, susanamedina@xr.earth wrote:

Hi Roc

Today I'm going to work a little bit on XR dialogue, then novel.

We need to bring our dialogue up to date, as things are happening so fast ... & the Summer Uprising ... Project Mushroom starting in five days' time! ... Good to hear about the secret location! Excellent! Wrote post on XR London Group suggesting locations along those lines, but it was probably decided much earlier. It's the logical thing to do!

I've just discovered that the pink used by XR is influenced by Paolozzi's 'angry' pink. So we can keep the Paolozzi bit ... Not so out of place, after all!

There are a few things I'd like to add to our dialogue ... I'll see where I can insert them ... Keywords:

SYM-BIO-SIS ... BIO-PHI-LIA ... LOVE ... RES-PON-SI-BI-LI-TY ... AL-TRU-ISM

> We urgently need to protect whales ... Whales accumulate approx. 33 tons of carbon dioxide in their bodies during their long lives, removing that carbon out of the atmosphere for centuries when they die and sink to the bottom of the ocean ... Kelp forests can sequester up to twenty times more carbon per acre than land, as macroalgae sink down to the deep-sea floor ... Mangroves can remove more carbon from the atmosphere than terrestrial forests, bamboos do so too ... Planting trees, rewilding ... though it takes thirty years for trees to begin to absorb a large amount of carbon dioxide. Loving and cherishing our ancient

forests and halting deforestation is vital, of course, as is loving and cherishing the oceans and our rivers, and all our species, and the insects ... Tackling peat burning ... Learning from Indigenous communities, the keepers of the earth ... Having fewer or no children, essential to reduce carbon footprint ... a meat-free diet ... a greener Green New Deal ... Insert some bad jokes? To speed up the transition, we'll start working on astral projection and quantum travel! If only cow burps could be converted into benign energy! ... The other day, thinking about the lack of pedestrianised areas in London and the need to transport things and disabled people we spoke about, I had this vision of a car-free Oxford Circus, just buses, bikes ... and rickshaws! I googled rickshaws and in India there are these new aerodynamic, ergonomic design rickshaws, electric! And if they could be promoted as ultracool, and as an alternative to the gym .... Anyway! It'd be interesting if products carried carbon footprint information. Like with food labelling, you have red, which is high sugar. Or better, and following the logic of the landscape, it could be like with the health warnings and gruesome pictures on tobacco products. There could be pictures of environmental destruction on dirty goods ... Pictures of devastating floods, tent-towns of refugees and moribund bears on billboards. Pictures of wildfires, burnt ancient trees and charred animals on the receipts from the petrol station ... Pictures of hundreds of starving reindeer, dead on a field, on flight tickets ... Close-ups of microplastics in our blood on beer labels and shellfish packets ... On some products, there could be a message saying: 'Instead of buying me, you may want to plant a few trees'.

See you tomorrow!

Miss Cellenea x

On Sunday 14 July 2019, at 11:05, rocsandford@xr.earth wrote:

Dear Susana,

The melting iceberg has been cooling off in the Gloucestershire countryside. But she is heading for London Fields presently, and Royal Courts tomorrow (but in the guise of a police liaison person). Stendhal, on Napoleon's March to Moscow, became a great connoisseur of fires. Likewise, I have become a great connoisseur of police. And set-piece scenes of conflict. It feels like living in Shakespeare. Or maybe Homer, really. Or Kleist. The epic has bled through the paper partition protecting it from the real, and drenched our lives.

Hope we meet! x

On Sunday 14 July 2019, at 19:35, susanamedina@xr.earth wrote:

What a lucky iceberg!

Was beginning to think you had melted away! Or your phone!

Would love to go to London Fields ... but can't.

Been editing our dialogue. Will continue today. Have been having, arghhhhh, PC troubleshooting! Strange! It might be sorted now. Fantastic that all these beautiful XR boats will be mushrooming across the UK.

Will be at the Royal Courts of Justice tomorrow ... How can ecocide not be made law? It's barbaric! Will message you if I don't see you .. x

On Monday 16 July 2019, at 15:38, susanamedina@xr.earth wrote:

Roc,

You OK?

Did you go to Bow early this morning?

... Five people arrested ... I hope you weren't one of them ... Pls answer asap!

... Saw the news. And then, the action pics on Twitter. A few hours later, as you weren't in the pics, started thinking, of course, Roc was arrested first thing in the morning!!!

I won't be able to go later to the XR Camp at Waterloo Millennium Green. I'll be looking after my mum from Saturday evening ... so, the pressure of doing lots of things before then! xooo

On Tuesday 17 July 2019, at 21:05, rocsandford@xr.earth wrote:

Dear Susana,

Head of Hammersmith Council said more or less exactly what we want to hear, after critical mass action. They are telling the truth, at least back to us. But they also need to act... x

On Wednesday 18 July 2019, at 11:35, susanamedina@xr.earth wrote:

OK see you Friday. Youth strike & XR march? Well ... good to hear about Hammersmith Council declaring Climate Emergency ... Argentina has just declared a Climate Emergency too! x

Something hilarious just happened. By mistake, eBay sent some transparent bra straps I bought to a fellow writer ... wrong address.

On Wednesday 18 July 2019, at 16:05, rocsandford@xr.earth wrote:

First Hammersmith and now Argentina! Fab! But a side of me'll believe it when I see it.

We are back home now taking it easy. Tomorrow I think I am going to Waterloo 9ish for a police briefing and then travelling in wake of XR boat to Parliament Square, and should be there all day. So yes, let's try to hook up after for a cider and a chat, something to look forward to, and if not, some time before you take over your mum. I might go away for the weekend but probably not.

Was it a 'male' writer who got the transparent bra straps? I hope so! Rx

On Wednesday 18 July 2019, at 19:35, susanamedina@xr.earth wrote:

Dear Roc,

Yes, a male writer, Richard Skinner. By mistake (long story), my eBay had his address as the primary delivery address ... not sure whether my name was on the invoice. As I didn't receive the item, I reported it as 'not received,' so he'll be getting another set ... but he's now been warned! Of course, he said it was a surreal moment. But just imagine, it could have been any item!

Tomorrow I'll be going to Requiem for a Dead Planet. I'm excited about this action. It's outside Northcliffe House, Derry St, where many newspapers have their offices. So we'll be there asking the media to tell the truth ... then the closing ceremony is in Parliament Square soon after. Maybe we could meet for a *tête-à-tête* afterwards or Saturday afternoon? ... I'll look for you during the closing ceremony ... message you x

Thursday 19 July: The Polly Higgins Boat, a Texting Interlude

R: *Where are you now? I'm still at Waterloo* x 11:29

S: *How come? The incessant rain? On my way to Requiem for a Dead Planet* x 12:35

S: *Hope you didn't get soaked! ... And it went well ...* 13:38

S: *In the company of skeletons & umbrellas asking mainstream media to tell the truth. Donnachadh McCarthy & Jon Fuller speaking.* 13:38

S: *It seems the closing ceremony in Parliament square has been cancelled...!!* 13:39

S: *Tell me where you'd like to meet* x 13:39

R: *Yes, voyage to Parliament cancelled because police wouldn't let ACT NOW Polly Higgins boat go—I'm staying with the boat until we figure it out. Yes, wet and cold! Hope you're not too wet. Let's play by ear where to meet—I may have to go via home to get dry* x 13:41

S: *Oh sorry to hear! Hope you're well ... poor you ...!* 13:46

S: *Swimming towards Parliament Sq* x 13:46

R: *I'm still with Polly Higgins at Waterloo. Are you at Parliament Square?* x 15:39

S: *Kilburn! Swimming home, have*

umbrella but freezing. 15:44

S: *How long are you likely to be there? Could change, get some warm clothes for you & come to Waterloo x* 15:44

R: *I'm going to swim home now to change — would you like to stop by on your way home? Or I could stop and say hello if you are in Parliament Sq? Or tomorrow afternoon? x* 15:57

S: *Helped the last tent in liquid Parliament Sq pack up. Warm now? x* 16:19

R: *Yes thank you—had a bath to warm up— maybe my last! Yes please swim by this eve for supper or we could meet tomorrow before your mum if better. This eve I'll prob go to bed 10ish because shattered x* 19:05

S: *Oh can imagine! I'll come briefly now, steered by the ghost of Polly Higgins ... no need to cook ... Will be there at 7.26 x* 19:06

Moby Dickery

On Friday, 26 July 2019, at 19:08, rocsandford@xr.earth wrote:

Dear Susana,

Great to hear you'll be coming along to the Moby-Dickery celebration of Herman Melville, raising funds for XR. Assuming David Collard, who is curating, is ok with this, if you wanted to come say something too that would be lovely. We have 15 minutes total. Here is what I wrote down to say. It's just a first draft which I haven't edited, and I may say something else completely.

Hello. David has very kindly offered to donate proceeds from this Evening's raffle to XR. I think many of the people here tonight were at *Finneganight*, his recent celebration of *Finnegans Wake*, so I will try not to repeat myself in my remarks about XR, except very briefly that XR is a Rebellion protesting government inaction on climate disaster and mass extinction, either of which is sufficient to make humans history in an extremely painful manner.

So, the first thing I'd like to say is it's not very green, hunting whales, is it? But in Melville's time, it must have felt as if the stock of whales was inexhaustible. We know better now, and the morality has switched. I'm old enough to have seen this happen over my lifetime, and I feel it can sometimes be unfair to judge behaviour carried out under an earlier morality by the standards of our own. So, I won't talk about whales. But it does occur to me that many of the routine and mundane activities which our society takes for granted, if they contribute to climate apocalypse or the sixth mass extinction, will very soon be regarded with the horror, repulsion, disgust and incredulity with which we regard whale slaughter, say, or slavery. As Auden says: 'Evil is unspectacular and always human, and shares our bed and eats at our own table.' What he doesn't say so far as I know is that's because evil is us.

Instead, I'll talk about the baby-blue XR boat, mascot of the London branch of the most recent Rebellion, which took place a week ago. The boat was called *Polly Higgins*, after a tradition of calling our boats after environmentalists. Polly was an open and loving person, a barrister who dropped out in order to sponsor a law of ecocide. And ecocide is the idea that just as you have war crimes, you can define a crime of destroying an ecosystem on which humans depend, and make that too a crime against humanity. Individuals will be liable to prosecution, so that the chairman of an oil company, for instance, will find themselves indicted, just as Albert Speer or Admiral Dönitz were. To become law, it just needs two thirds of countries to ratify it. The Pacific island nations who are sinking as we speak are jumping on board and I'm hoping, in my optimistic moments, that this will happen fairly quickly. Polly suddenly sickened a few months ago, and died during the Easter Rebellion—I heard when I was on Waterloo bridge—so it was very moving to have this boat named after her.

So, we had this baby-blue boat, the *Polly Higgins*, and our aim was to use it to block the Strand outside the Royal Courts of Justice, to focus the minds of the legal establishment on the merits of a law of ecocide. How it works is we talk to the police before a protest and tell them what we have in mind. On this occasion we didn't tell them we had a boat, we said it was a mushroom. They guessed it wasn't a mushroom, and were running sweepstakes as to what it actually would be. One officer told me he thought it would be an orange biplane, another an open-topped bus with a big number written on the side. One guessed it would be another hot-pink boat, and he was nearly right. They were pestering me like children for the secret. In the event, it was a baby-blue boat, the *Polly Higgins*, brilliantly refitted and skippered by a nautical rebel.

The police have lost much of the sanction of fear of arrest, which some XR people, given our scary climate predicament, see as a badge of supreme honour, so the police kind of have to just listen to what we want to tell them. But when they saw a baby-blue boat, imperfectly hidden under a tarp, being towed across Blackfriars Bridge, they had their suspicions, and stopped it. We just said, okay, if we must, we will block Blackfriars Bridge instead, so then they let it go again, and we parked it in front of the Royal Courts. That all went well, and in the end, nobody got arrested. At the end of the day we went in a very slow procession across Waterloo Bridge, which me and Susana here have a soft spot for, and parked-up in Waterloo.

That was all fine until Friday, when there was a bit of a stand-off between the police and the rebels. The assistant commissioner got up at 5:21 am on Friday morning to issue an order that, if the boat (or the massive pink dodo we also had with us) were to join a procession to Parliament Square as planned, it would be seized, and everyone involved arrested. Some rebels were jumping at this possibility. So, both the police and the rebels were angling for the boat, and my job, with some other rebels, was to hold them both off as long as possible. Because another group also wanted the boat, having been tipped off by Clive Russell, one of the designers behind XR's stunning iconography, and this was the National Maritime Museum, or NMM. So, I spent Friday soaking wet, haggling with both police and rebels, playing for time, until, amazingly, an NMM curator and a marine surveyor suddenly emerged from the pouring rain, checked the boat didn't have any asbestos for bureaucratic health and safety reasons, and then climbed into the tow truck with the nautical skipper and drove away into a curtain of rain, leaving both police and rebels empty-handed. NMM had moved with incredible nimbleness for a cultural bureaucracy, a sign perhaps of how desperate they were for it.

So, this revolutionary boat will now take its place in the vicinity of Inigo Jones's Queen's House—that revolutionary building. At the last minute (as I knew would happen), a traffic policeman complained about the stepped mast overhanging the back of the boat being a hazard to HGVs. So, I took off my baby-blue vest and Polly's nimble skipper, who had navigated her surely through the shoals of the Strand and Waterloo, hung that on the end of the mast. And the boat sailed off down The Cut and out into history, my vest flapping out behind like a sodden Jolly Roger. That all felt important—that Rebellion should get mainstream cultural endorsement and so be progressively legitimised, and all the people visiting Greenwich will see the boat, wonder who Polly was, and maybe bother to find out. As Miles puts it: 'it's a culture war, and if it's a culture war, we've won.' Obviously, this kind of cultural legitimation won't suit our opposite numbers in the fossil fuel and car and aviation industries, and their employees in governments and media, and we are expecting a rougher ride at the next major phase of the Rebellion, which starts on October 7th. All are welcome by the way, and judging how things have been so far, you are unlikely to get arrested if you don't want to be. It really is worth being part of—like the events of '68, or the Selma marches—imagine having the opportunity to take part in those! But this is like that, only more, because 'we are life defending itself'. So, thank you again David for your generosity in supporting XR.

On Friday, 26 July 2019, at 21:07, susanamedina@xr.earth wrote:

Hi Pond Rebel,

Here been a bit ZZZZZZ.

Glad you finished *Philosophical Toys* ... Merci for message and compliments, yes, we'll talk about it!

What you've written for this evening is good ... So, don't know what I could add, given the time limit and short notice (I know you mentioned it when we met two days ago, thank you for thinking about me!) I mainly wanted to talk about ecocide, but you're covering it ... If I do say something at the *Moby-Dickery* event it'd be along these lines:

> Moby-Dick is about lordship over nature. And now the time has come to transcend this type of lordship ... W. H. Auden said something like 'The trouble with fighting evil is it generates evil. And there's no time to create beauty.' (Quote stolen from Roc's dodgy memory-banks.) In most of its actions, XR creates beauty. It creates fun. XR has a very strong sense of the importance of art in climate activism. In most actions, there are collective performances, and intellectually stimulating talks. Last week, it was the Summer Uprising. We parked the Polly Higgins

ACT NOW baby-blue boat outside The Royal Courts of Justice. A flag which read MAKE ECOCIDE LAW was raised half-mast by a dancer, while a violinist played music. It was beautiful. Many other beautiful performances and fascinating talks followed.

A couple of days later, we did Requiem for a Dead Planet, all rebels dressed in black, and there were a couple of skeletons sitting on office chairs reading the *Daily Mail* outside the offices of the *Independent*, the *Daily Mail*, the *Mail on Sunday*, *London Live*, the *Evening Standard* and the *Metro*. The demand was for them to TELL THE TRUTH and stop high-carbon advertising (cars, flights, cruises), which is a mammoth contradiction with some of the papers that regularly cover climate change. We ended the action with a die-in. Preparing for this action yielded good results, with the *Independent* and *ITV* agreeing to meet up with climate activists. You might not be aware, but it is only due to a lot of pressure, hard work and negotiating from activists, that there is more media coverage, such as *ITV's* new regular slot on the 10pm news to highlight the devastating climate crisis happening right now. Of course, *Channel 4* is good at covering it. But climate change deniers dominate YouTube searches on global warming. And the coming together of all these ecological movements is leading to an increase in disinformation campaigns and climate science denial data wars funded by big money. The pressure has to be kept up. We have to broadcast the fact that the public is not being told that climate change and loss of biodiversity are the greatest threats humanity has ever faced, nor about the urgent measures necessary to keep the planet below 1.5 C. We need to rebel for life.

We're doing all sorts of actions to raise awareness about the issues ruining our planet irreversibly. Anyone can design an action. I would love to see some of you in these actions. Many of them are beautiful, moving. As artists and writers, we can all create art for these actions.

Will be raining around 6.00 ... So pleased the event is in the Tin Church! Didn't know they were doing events there ... must be recent!

Will wear mythological XR skirt. Will try to get there a bit earlier.

See you there ...

Sxooo

August 2019 Emails: Dear Angelus Novus

You have to act as if it were possible to radically transform the world. And you have to do it all the time. *Angela Davies*

On Saturday, 3 August 2019, at 14:24, susanamedina@xr.earth wrote:

Allo Roc,

How are you? The sheep Damien Hirst used for art piece, was yours, yes?

Well, thank you for mini-meal (owe you 3 mini-meals with lots of cider … and almonds) and, above all, thank you for the fig from your tree!

Here, attached, ze file of ze dialogue. Follow the hashtags and I have highlighted in green repetition and re-insertation, so, once neated up and … approved … you can put it back in black. It'd be good to include some fiction in the dialogue, interpolations and bifurcations. What do you say? Do you have any relevant pieces?

Have a lovely day, Sx

PS: Picked up my mum from Soho yesterday evening … amazing how many rickshaws around, but for tourists! … Just read that the amount of heat transferred into the oceans during the last twenty-five years equals 3.6 billion Hiroshima atom-bomb explosions.

On Saturday, 3 August 2019, at 22:08, rocsandford@xr.earth wrote:

Hey Susana,

Good idea about the fiction. The creative non-fiction tip can be drab or tart. Actually in our case it's more *experimental* non-fiction. So here is a very short homage to Heinrich von Kleist I wrote many years ago as an artwork in an exhibition. It's called *Siege of the Byzantines*. It isn't bright and dark, like your *Dear Angelus Novus*, but only dark, and I am sorry. But I was surrounded everywhere by people who thought I was crazy to be panicking about climate disaster, and I was trying to find a way to shock them into thinking about it. It didn't work. Perhaps it's too extreme. Some people were completely mystified and kept asking me what it meant, and some of those who understood what it meant never talked to me again ...

SIEGE OF THE BYZANTINES

In 1085 Robert Guiskard, known as 'the weasel', besieged the Byzantines, whilst his own knights and the city's garrison were dying of plague. He himself died before the city, already a necropolis, could capitulate.

In 1803 Heinrich von Kleist burned *Robert Guiskard*, his play on the futility of this siege of the dead by the dying, which Wieland had compared with Sophocles and Shakespeare. 'I read my work over, rejected it, and burned it. This is the end', he said. Some years later, after brandy and coffee served to them on the beach of the Kleiner Wannsee, Kleist shot first his dear friend Frau Vogel, and then himself.

My own trial, too, had this futile zombie quality: the dying comfort the dead. And I too had still work to do. But the CEOs & CFOs of big oil and the airlines and of course the paid deniers were all strung up by now, together with their lovers, husbands, kids, each dangling from their feet like il Duce and Clara. Bled, gralloched and clinking, freeze-dried in the perma-gale, we call them the chimes. As in wind-chimes, war-chimes, carbon-chimes, lunch-chimes, dinner-chimes.

Now the court was mopping up the small fry. The charge was that I had travelled by air and in my grand-aunt's car. This I did not deny, claiming in defence that I did not know. Nobody knew, in those days, what was happening; everyone was complicit, there was nothing illegal about travelling by air or by car. I did not know. I did not know.

But in the eyes of the court, ignorance is no defence; my not knowing, they said, was wilful denial. The denial of the goy who, on taking the newly vacant but delicately furnished flat in Frankfurt an der Oder, whose shivering geraniums splash scarlet petals on white carpets, did not know that *Arbeit Macht Frei*.

I did not know, said the court, because I did not care to know. And not caring to know, but travelling by air and car all the same, were the crime with which I was charged. Did I understand? 'I am not a bad person,' I told the court, 'it is just that I did not know.' The clerks and ushers of the court, and even the advocates, and even my judge, and even the courtroom cleaner had not known either—they too await their summons, while the court's walls hold, and the lunch-chimes last.

A little dark, I know!

As for the dialogue, it's looking great. I have gone through and made some corrections, and I will have another look at it tomorrow x Roc

On Tuesday, 6 August 2019, 10:12, susanamedina@xr.earth wrote:

Dear Melting Iceberg,

Worried about you, as July was the hottest month ever recorded on Earth. July has rewritten climate history. Arctic permafrost isn't thawing gradually, as scientists predicted. It's thawing almost overnight ... And it contains twice as much carbon as that currently destroying the atmosphere of the planet!

We can have *The Siege of the Byzantines* as part of the final emails ... I loved the piece, with its darkness, macabre overtones and deadpan wisdom. Kafka meets Lovecraft via Borges. I like the way it's framed with the dead and the dying, and the fitting, over-the-millennia references to the bizarre siege at the beginning. Didn't know Kleist committed suicide with his friend. He wrote a beautiful essay on marionettes ... which is part of one of my favourite books, a very small blue book called *Essays on Dolls*.

When are you going back to Gometra? Will miss you! It's so absurd I'll be at the Edinburgh Fringe Festival with XR Scotland, and it'd be so nice to hop to Gometra on my way back ... and yet, not the right time, what with all the recent family holidays, readings, and my novel impatiently waiting for me after so many interruptions! Sx

On Saturday, 10 August 2019, at 15:41, rocsandford@xr.earth wrote:

Dear Susana,

I have already gone to Gometra! It is very wild here and I am thinking of you on the serene floating isle of cats that is Kilburn.

The waves are enormous, the wind is grating on the roof, the rain is rattling the windows, and I have developed all sorts of strange insatiable cravings—chocolate pudding, red wine, olives. Please eat and drink some for me.

On the way here from London, there were floods, and the train had to plough through water like the train in *Spirited Away*. It is strange when a train becomes a boat—two mythologies couple. We crossed a bridge with a fierce, bright brown river with white standing waves breaking in it, always in the same place, which had flooded a wood.

And my dear friend Gerry Dalton died last week. He made the guerrilla outsider artist sculpture garden along the canal, which I've described as portraying the dreams and subconscious of history itself. And now he's gone, the British Museum seems to be suddenly interested in his work (I may have misunderstood—my friend Sasha texted me opaquely that she had talked to a curator there, but could be a different museum). As he was dying, I told him he was very much loved, and was an important artist. He was wearing an oxygen mask, like an astronaut. He said 'I'm done for, keep the garden.' He waited until his niece got back from Ireland to say goodbye, and then he died. His family have asked me to help carry his coffin, which made me cry. I'm going to store his work in my house until we can figure out something. It reminds me of my friend Magouche, who when she was widowed, stored her husband Arshile Gorky's canvases under her bed. It turned out he had helped to invent something called Abstract Expressionism, and every museum of modern art had to have one. But if lovely Gerry gets famous now, it's a little sad that he just missed it.

Here we are quite cozy. But everyone is being really lazy about cutting wood so we have no fire. I feel reset, so that I could come to London a new being, with new energy. It is good being here. But at the same time, not as good as normal because there are XR things that I should have done and have not yet done, so I am feeling guilty and pressurised.

Sending lots of love dear Susana. I hope the novel is nearly finished, I am longing to see it when the time comes. And please tell me how the XR Edinburgh Festival went x Roc

On Monday, 12 August 2019, at 15:13, susanamedina@xr.earth wrote:

Dear Roc,

Back in Ithaca?

I'm sorry your friend Gerry has died. A hug from here, and it's good to hear his work is in good hands and that his family appreciates you too. The picture you send me of his work is intriguing.

First two days in Edinburgh pissing down with rain, so worked on novel. It was great meeting Scottish Rebels, and getting to know XR Scotland. I really like the Scots. My host was young and perky, and wore a short top that revealed her belly button, combined with a skirt showing hairy legs … The XR series of events at Summerhall were fascinating, excellent performances & events … & art. They screened *This changes everything*, based on Naomi Klein's book. The exhibition space wasn't that big, mainly wall space. There was this wall piece I really enjoyed: everyday single-plastics filled with black ink. It conveyed with simplicity how polluting single-plastics are!

Good to hear you'll come back a new being. It's amazing how nature and rest replenishes one … And of course, Gometra is pure nature, so that must be intensely healing.

Last night, I had a devilishly dark chocolate soya dessert … the Alpro ones … You know them? My favourite chocolate pudding. Also, I had two figs that looked like really big olives, so following your instructions almost to the letter … Red wine will have to wait.

Here's sunny and might go to the garden now, quality time with the foxes.

Looking forward to re-configured you.

Regards to the waves Sx

On Tuesday, 13 August 2019, at 17:23, rocsandford@xr.earth wrote:

Thank you, dear Susana

Well yes, here it feels like Ithaca—same primitive wholesomeness!

But there in London, perhaps, with all that's happening, more like Troy!

I see on the news pictures of Lazer glued to the Brazilian Embassy. I don't know if he was arrested. There are pictures of him lying on the ground surrounded by police, manacled, so I suppose he was, but he looks okay. I'm worried but it also makes me feel elated he is so brave. It's an action he did with his friend Fox and others to protest the burning of the Amazon—something that risks killing us all. Roc x

On Tuesday 13 August 2019, at 21:14 susanamedina@xr.earth wrote:

Dear Roc

Hope brave Lazer is fine ... you must have heard from him by now?

Wanted to go to the XR action at the Brazilian Embassy, as so important and timely! Saw pics, and yes, saw Lazer in the *Guardian* and other papers being carried by four policemen, red paint all over his hands and shoe soles. It's a good picture. It reminded me you once said your children are your novels. Court case soon? ... Of course, it's Bolsonaro et al who should be arrested and imprisoned.

I have the flu! It slowly crept up on me on this morning, then spent a few hours on dialogue and my novel, then started to feel kaput ... Undoubtedly, the Scottish flu! Sx

PS: Forgot to tell you that while in Edinburgh, I went to the Scottish National Gallery of Modern Art ... and surprise, surprise there's a recreation of Paolozzi's London studio, full of his models and maquettes, and he made a substantial amount of cast plaster models of animals ... so, your dog is not so un-Paolozzi after all!

On Wednesday, 14 August 2019, at 8:02, rocsandford@xr.earth wrote:

Dear Susana

You poor thing! Flu is horrible. Sending you flu repellent, optimism and happiness enclosed in this email. I hope you can rest completely until you are better, waited on by those fine cats Magic and Little One.

Lazer is fine. It was only that I found the picture of him lying shackled on the ground amidst the police people scary.

Sending lots of love from Gometra x Roc

On Sunday, 18 August 2019, at 11:19, susanamedina@xr.earth wrote:

Bonjour!

How are you? Is it warm in Gometra?

Merci for flu antidote ... I was finally back at my desk yesterday ... Very proud of Lazer, tell him pls and rather depressed about the Amazon burning et al.

... Will write soon!

Regards to fauna and tribe xooo

On Sunday, 18 August 2019, at 12:04, rocsandford@xr.earth wrote:

Hola Susana,

So glad you are in business again—flu can be so depressing and miserable! x Roc

On Thursday, 22 August 2019, at 11:19, susanamedina@xr.earth wrote:

Roc,

Been editing this chapter, 'Hotel Kafka', in my novel. A good day ... will finish tomorrow, then our dialogue ... vital to finish it and get it out ... I was thinking when we started the recordings, Greta Thunberg was barely known, and now she's getting all these awards, and Fridays for Future have really taken off. It's so inspiring! And Greta, magnificent! I also love the way she talks about Asperger's syndrome as her superpower ... And was also thinking, when we started, the idea was to do a series of magazine interviews, and now ... We have a book!?

That'll mean more work, of course! Well, hope you're having a good rest and that your books don't take precedence over enjoying the fresh air and the sheer massage of nature ... I suspect that's probably the case?

... And now, a bit of garden-meadow with foxes x

On Friday, 23 August 2019, at 19:04, rocsandford@xr.earth wrote:

Dear Susana

Yes, nature here is quite amazing. But also a little sad, because it is quite tough to do anything.

Yesterday we dragged a broken boat a mile so as to use it for our protest on Sunday. We are planning to block a little bridge with it. It was sad in a way, because it was so hard to drag it. It feels like you are up against forces bigger than you. But the young people have painted it beautifully with *ACT NOW* and *HOPE ISLAND*.

Otherwise we are quite cozy and cooking delicious food.

As to Greta, I forgot to tell you that I was in Stockholm staying with my friend Frida in the summer of 2018. Around the beginning of August, I got on a train back to London. But I saw on Twitter a young girl had gone to sit in front of the Swedish Parliament. Had I not got on my train, I would have gone to sit beside her, but I told Frida who was still there, to go sit beside her. That was Greta's first few days of striking, and I missed out on them!

Sending lots of love from Gometra x Roc

On Sunday, 25 August 2019, at 21:34, susanamedina@xr.earth wrote:

Dear Roc,

Just saw photos of the XR painted boat, merci …! Excellent! Congratulations to the Gometra Rebels! Great to see the green XR flag flying tall! The last pic is so beautiful with the reflection on the water of all the rebels across the bridge! One of my favourite XR actions! xooo

PS: My latest idea is to insert 'Dear Angelus Novus,' the piece I read at the Rebellion, at the beginning, as part of the emails … so, it begins with some art … If you like this idea, can you pls make up an email where you say 'why don't we include it?' Or better, can you make up an email/s (or add to an existing one) where I suggest including your *Byzantines* piece (include your friends' reactions you mention) and you suggest including some of my work?

On Friday, 30 August 2019, 15:41 BST, rocsandford@xr.earth wrote:

Dear Susana,

All well with me. So, as planned, we had the protest—occupied our tiny bridge from Gometra to Ulva with a brightly painted boat—very successful—much coverage in the National Press, I will send cuttings. In the last section of the dialogue I was thinking of maybe putting in a little bit about the protest—

HOPE ISLAND

All of us on Gometra (pop. 8) occupied the little bridge between the Isle of Gometra and its neighbour Ulva, and blocked it with a boat, in solidarity with the islands like Fiji and the Solomon Islands where real people with lovers and friends and secrets of their own are already dying because of the climate and ecological apocalypse. On the boat was written ACT NOW and HOPE ISLAND. Then we all got into the boat and waited. But nobody came. Eventually a Plaid Cymru councillor and his friend, who were on holiday, wandered by. They got into the boat with us. I'd forgotten to ring the police, so no-one was arrested. But the Scottish press went mad. People are obsessed with islands, and besides, there was an element of the absurd in our action, occupying a bridge which hardly anyone wants to cross. Everyone understands the language of the absurd, because it's the foundation of both nationalism and religion.

A few days later we had our theatre festival. There were some very beautiful plays. This was one of my pieces: it's short. It's called *Birds*. It starts with a mother (played by me) pushing a child (played by Blue) in a pushchair, and the mother says—

—When mummy was a little girl there used to be birds!
—Kewl!
—Yes pet. We would see them just there.
—Wicked!
—Yes …
—Mummy, why are you crying?
—(Voice blinded by tears) It's okay, it's okay.
—And mummy?
—Yes pet?
—What are birds?

And I got big media coverage too for my friend's salmon farm protest—very pleased!

Sorry about the long silence—I got so rushed that I stopped dwelling on my friends for far too long. But really looking forward to hearing your news and seeing you.

So, sending you lots of love from a train now rushing down the spine of England x ooo Roc

On Saturday, 1 September 2019, at 15:41, rocsandford@xr.earth wrote:

Chère Petite Vilaine,

Now I'm in London. Rather shocking, all these people.

I didn't use your original idea to make up an email where you suggest including *my* piece, because I thought your email suggesting that was already good enough. So, as you will already have seen, I have slipped your email into the dialogue earlier on. And now, at last, I'll be sending you next *my* made-up email asking you if we can include *Dear Angelus Novus*.

Looking forward to our next meeting. Roc x

On Sunday, 2 September 2019, at 08:12, rocsandford@xr.earth wrote:

Dear Susana,

Gr8x. Black Lion Weds 6ish. And thank you for that lovely video at the XR pavilion at the Edinburgh Festival, containing nested within it as backdrop, a projection of your reading from the Pink Boat at Oxford Circus!

So why don't we include *Dear Angelus Novus* at the end of the dialogue? Send me the latest version and I'll add it to the very end of the dialogue file.

It's a monument to what is happening, what is and what will be, and what should. I love the way it is both bright and dark, and brighter than it is dark. We now know, only when it is almost too late, but not quite too late, that earth was Eden, and the forbidden fruit which grew on the tree of life was fossil fuels, but really evil in general. And we are still prospecting for the other tree, the tree of knowledge, so as to fell it and make it into sawdust.

As for my piece, *Siege of the Byzantines*, it is just dark, and darker than it is dark. No wonder no one will talk to me after reading it. It is frozen, whilst yours is molten.

It makes me think of this: while he was still a student and still in what he called the shameful lowlands of literature, Kafka wrote to his schoolfriend Oskar Pollak—

> I think we ought to read only the kind of books that wound or stab us. If the book we're reading doesn't wake us up with a blow to the head, what are we reading for? So that it will make us happy, as you write? Good Lord, we would be happy precisely if we had no books, and the kind of books that make us happy are the kind we could write ourselves if we had to. But we need books that affect us like a disaster, that grieve us deeply, like the death of someone we loved more than ourselves, like being banished into forests far from everyone, like a suicide. A book must be the axe for the frozen sea within us. That is my belief.

Did you know that Nabokov, who didn't read Kafka until after Kafka died, said when he saw Kafka's photo something like this—

> My God! It's the man who used to sit opposite me every day on the U-Bahn. He always got off at the same stop. He—was going to see his mistress!

And did you know that Nabokov, who was a lepidopterist, figured out what kind of creature Gregor Samsa had become, and that he had wings hidden under his wing case, and had he only known it, could have flown away.

With love from your friend, the melting iceberg x ooo x

On Tuesday, 3 September 2019, at 09:19, susanamedina@xr.earth wrote:

Have had a quick look at the dialogue, nice you insert new lit quotes … especially lepidopterist Nabokov's insight about Gregor Samsa's ignorance, which gives us hope … I've changed my mind. *Dear Angelus Novus* should go at the beginning? So here, my dear melting iceberg, is the updated version of the dialogue. As a title for the book, do you like *We Are the Asteroid, We Are the Dinosaurs?* ... Thinking we need less dystopian writing about the emergency, googled novels about ecological utopia and came across *Ecotopia*, by Ernest Callenbach, published in 1975, a bestseller. I suppose most environmentalists must know about it ... I didn't, but then, I'm a neophyte. Northern California, Oregon and Washington secede to create an ecosystem, the perfect balance between humans and the environment. It's good, prescient! Written as a report by a journalist, a kind of travelogue ... Ecotopia's inhabitants have some weird customs, but, largely, it portrays the kind of society we need to become to avert societal collapse. It's so thorough when it comes to solutions, and it embraces technology selectively ... There are no deaths from air and chemical pollution, ecocide is law, and economy acknowledges all costs, so it becomes a subset of ecology ... free electric transport ... they worship trees, have ecotopian plastics derived from plants, no flights can cross their territory, manufactured items are durable and self-fixable. They're fond of history, especially 'industrial history' and its crimes, and they have museum displays of our barbarism ... Looking forward to tomorrow! Sxooo

PS: I recently read *The Great Derangement* (2016) by Amitav Gosh ... It's a necessary and urgent book, brilliant, really, though I don't entirely agree with some of his arguments ... Of course, there are lots of excellent points, namely that the literary mainstream remains unaware of the crisis ... He says:

> When future generations look back upon the Great Derangement they will certainly blame the leaders and politicians of this time for their failure to address the climate crisis. But they may well hold artists and writers to be equally culpable—for the imagining of possibilities is not, after all, the job of politicians and bureaucrats.

True, but then lots of land artists in the 70s tried to engage us in a dialogue with nature (Suzi Gablik's lovely *The Reenchantment of Art* (1992) discusses wonderful ecological art projects) and there are so many poets, not included, as his focus is on realist fiction ... He doesn't engage with science fiction. *Ecotopia* is not mentioned ... perhaps it wasn't deemed 'literary' enough? ... Italo Calvino deals with ecological issues, and he's comically critical of post-industrial life in his short stories in *Marcovaldo* ... would love to re-read it, as it's a bit hazy in my mind ... Octavio Paz embraces the inherent connection between nature and human psyche in *The Monkey Grammarian* (1974) ... Ballard imagines a flooded world in *The Drowned World* (1962) and *The Terminal Beach* (1964) may contain some jewels? And, there are so many more books we might not be aware of ... Here, looking forward to reading *The Overstory* by Richard Powers, which was published recently. And, on another note, *Doughnut Economics: Seven Ways to Think Like a 21st-Century Economist*, by economist Kate Raworth, who writes about respecting the limits of the planet's resources and eradicating global poverty.

December 2019 Emails: The October Rebellion

On Exactitude in Science

... In that Empire, the Art of Cartography attained such Perfection that the map of a single Province occupied the entirety of a City, and the map of the Empire, the entirety of a Province. In time, those Unconscionable Maps no longer satisfied, and the Cartographers Guilds struck a Map of the Empire whose size was that of the Empire, and which coincided point for point with it. The following Generations, who were not so fond of the Study of Cartography as their Forebears had been, saw that that vast Map was Useless, and not without some Pitilessness was it, that they delivered it up to the Inclemencies of Sun and Winters. In the Deserts of the West, still today, there are Tattered Ruins of that Map, inhabited by Animals and Beggars; in all the Land there is no other Relic of the Disciplines of Geography. Suárez Miranda, Viajes de varones prudentes, Libro IV, Cap XLV, Lérida, 1658.
Jorge Luis Borges

On Saturday, 21 December 2019, at 21:12, rocsandford@xr.earth wrote:

Querida Susana,

Thank you for the Trafalgar Sq Rhapsody draft! And you have asked me to write, too, about the October Rebellion.

I find it harder to write about than the April Rebellion.

October Rebellion

In the April Rebellion, the sun drilled down on Waterloo Bridge, where I spent most of the time—by day it was too hot, even in the shade of the groves which had suddenly sprung up on the blacktop. There were real bees, drawn to the blossom on our cherry trees. There was the portable pond I built on the southbound carriageway, with its sleeping bag-filled tent in which you were supposed to lie and watch the water—a modern Walden. My message was that there are better uses for roads than driving on. At night there was a moon, and stars, and languid music on a distant guitar. You could look from the unzipped entrance of your tent down the Thames at the jelly-dome of St Paul's trembling there weightlessly, and upriver at the dreaming spires of the Palace of Westminster, inflected by the air shimmering above the water. Within a few hours we had converted one of the most horrible places on earth to one of the loveliest.

And as if silently and somewhere else, we were also being battered by endless waves of police in their *gilets jaunes*, as they tried to take back the bridge so as to open it up again to boring, poisonous traffic. But they didn't have the bandwidth to arrest us all—not enough cells, not enough vans—there were too many of us—and they were reluctant, presumably for PR reasons, to use a London bus to take us on a mystery tour to a stadium or a church. Or even a mass grave. That may yet happen, and when it happens, it will neither look, nor be, good. We, meanwhile, even in this state of strange tranquillity, swept by the seas of police, were all the same wearied by the perpetual rattling of a police helicopter, always overhead.

I spent some of my time chained to the driveshaft underneath the slewed lorry we had first used to block the bridge, to make it hard for the police to take it away—in a state of deep serenity, at the silent eye of the storm—the desert mothers and fathers came to mind. So the April rebellion itself had high aesthetic unity, a colouring of its own, and whatever happened to me within it had colourful unity too, superimposed on the rebellion.

October was different. My child Blue, with Fox and three other friends, was arrested on top of a scaffold blocking the Strand on the first day, and held in solitary for 27 hours in Barking and Dagenham custody centre, the custodial version of a Big Yellow Storage depot, on a sinister industrial estate far out on London's ragged eastern fringes. It's the kind of landscape J. G. Ballard loved. I went to claim her back. When Blue came out she wouldn't speak, even to me, was just silent with her head down, and once we got outside she took off her shoes and dragged her small white feet through the wet grass. There was a tiny dark-age nunnery, on the muddy banks of Barking Creek, surrounded by a halo of grass with Blue dragging her white feet through it, and then whirling all around us, heartless roads and warehouses.

The glistening slate-blue mud of the creek symbolised wildness; and the grass of the dark-age nunnery, domesticity; and the freeways to nowhere and the ranked, boxy warehouses, all the horror and bleakness of materialism and the ending of the universe.

It made me remember that story I so love, told me by an elderly primatologist many years ago, of how she was trying to protect the mountain gorillas in a war zone which had been rubber-stamped in blood-red on their misty, magical Eden—their Olympus even! She got a call from a sergeant in a police station which was being used as a barracks. He took her past muttering soldiers and down the row of cells and opened one—and in the corner, squatting down with her face to the wall, making herself tiny and invisible, was an adolescent gorilla the soldiers had captured for bushmeat. The primatologist emitted what she called a burp vocalisation, which is how gorillas say hello, and the gorilla in one revolving leap ended up with her arms and legs wrapped round the primatologist's torso, and her face buried in her breasts. They set off walking hand in hand back to gorilla Eden.

Eating gorillas is like eating super-intelligent and sensitive dodos. Maybe the sergeant understood this. Maybe the soldiers were hungry. But these are all projections. All I know is what she told me.

The primatologist told me another story I love—she wanted to understand the diet of the silverbacks, the Kong-sized mature male gorillas who led the gorilla passel—and she spent all day following one, collecting (dogged as Ophelia) exactly the simples and herbs he collected. At the end of the day she had an enormous bunch she was going to analyse, but the gorilla approached her, took it appreciatively and, his face slightly raised, savouring each leaf, he ate it. I've just looked on the web to find the primatologist, because I've forgotten her name, though I'm sure it's in my notebook, but with that kind of frisson on my crest and behind my eyes which always betrays that spirits are lurking, I learn that if I have the right one, she herself was murdered, soon after our conversation, by the soldiers. Presumably for bushmeat. We are used to stories like this happening elsewhere, but we must learn, if we don't stop venting carbon into heaven, that they will also happen here, and you and I will only live long enough to die in this way too.

So Blue came out, traumatised by police intimidation and guilt-tripping—threats of being 'reluctantly' forced to strip-search her, refusal to allow her to make her lawyer-call, not giving her water, alleging random rapists would be busily raping whilst the police were tied up ministering to her self-indulgent needs, switching off her bell so she couldn't call for help, yet simultaneously putting her on suicide watch and waking her all the time with intrusive inspections. So on. Her trauma fed through to me, and as we do, self-importantly, I felt she was silently raging at me.

They said they were going to charge her with theft of the scaffolding tower, which was ridiculous—if you intend to steal something you don't place it in the midst of the largest concentration of police in Europe, and besides she had not brought it to the square, she'd just climbed up it. It was her birthday that night, so without knowing the time she didn't know how old she was. They kept saying 'How old are you?'; she kept replying 'What time is it?'; which unfortunately wound them up to a pitch of spitefulness. And then, once they had let me in to see her, her interview had a dark comedy, in that the windowless charge-room lights on their timer kept going out, and the film of the interview, made for the court, is regularly plunged into total darkness with, when the lights at last come back on, me disclosed still leaping and waving wildly so as to trigger the motion-sensor. Blue had to write a statement, the first line of which is 'Today is my seventeenth birthday. I've spent it in a cell.' When we finally got back from the custody centre, late that night, and wormed our way past the police back into Trafalgar Square, there was a cake for Blue, and she blew out her candles sitting on the flags at the foot of Nelson's Column, surrounded by concentric rings of rebels and police.

The police were clearly being squeezed by the politicians, and so making mistakes. When we went in to tell them our plans before the October Rebellion started—as you know, we have a policy of radical transparency, and usually tell them what we have in mind—they just looked deeply uncomfortable, and the higher-ups said it was 'totally unacceptable!', and sulked. Going up in the lift to meet them in the Police HQ in Lambeth—which is a converted multi-story carpark—in this enormous stainless steel lift, like those lifts you see in hospitals which are big enough for an automobile, I had felt an agonising dread, knowing that our lawful right to peaceful protest could easily curdle, and this very lift become a prelude to torture and disappearance. I remembered the movie *Brazil*. And the autobiography I once read of an Argentinian whose job it was to push living activists out of an aeroplane over the sea. And even thought of my godfather Xan Fielding who as a spy had been picked up with a friend in occupied France because he was caught carrying too much money, but who was sprung by another spy, Christine Granville, who—accounts differ—either came and screamed at the Gestapo, playing Xan's friend's belligerent wife, or else bribed their captors to release them. Xan thought he was being led out to be shot, but instead it was to her fuming face and waiting car.

One of the biggest police mistakes was, as I'm sure you remember, to issue what is called a Section 14 order that no two XR *sympathisers* could gather together anywhere in London—on the back of which they made hundreds of arrests. The courts then ruled this order unlawful, meaning that the police became retrospectively guilty of wrongful arrest and false imprisonment on an impressive scale, and took a massive PR and confidence hit. XR likewise took a PR hit when an attempt to immobilise an underground train by climbing on the roof resulted in violence from angry passengers. This action had been opposed by most of XR, but because of XR's autonomous structure, had gone ahead. A further PR mistake on the part of the authorities was, at the instigation of their handlers in oil & gas, to attempt to brand XR, whose core belief and practice is non-violence, as terrorists.

So there was more disruption of XR's right to peaceful protest than usual—our disabled facilities were confiscated, together with our stainless kitchen sink—I filmed that, gleaming behind its cordon of police. They had raided our warehouse and taken our celebrated pink cushions even before the rebellion began—and they kept going for our infrastructure, having realised perhaps that by now it was too late to win by trying to arrest us all—those days were gone, we were too many. It rained, people got wet, we had lost our tents and our dry clothes, and morale was low, which was the police's cunning plan. I heard someone say they had never before spent two weeks with wet feet, and never intended to again.

We started off October with twelve London sites—but quickly lost many of them. The police were trying to corral us back into Trafalgar Square. Give us a fall-back position, and then mop us up there.

I spent the succeeding days liaising with the police; or else at Southwark Crown Court, where my son Lazer was being tried for glueing himself to the Brazilian Embassy to protest destruction of the Amazonian rainforest and murder of its Indigenous inhabitants; or else performing my protest art-piece. Trafalgar Square's theme was Burning Earth, about the fall-out of the climate and ecological disaster. I put a black pyramid I had built, representing the afterlife, into one of the Trafalgar Square fountains having, beforehand, progressed around the protest inside it. People *loved* the pyramid. Even some of the police were amused, but some of them had a sense of humour failure and started off down the arrest pathway—and I watched through my peephole from the safety of its interior as they clocked the logistical difficulties involved in arresting a motile black pyramid. On each occasion I was able to scuttle away, leaving them indignant but demoralised, and presumably cheering themselves up by preparing identikit pictures of a fishy tetrahedroid they wished to interview in connection with their enquiries.

The rebellion was so chaotic that I lost the pyramid several times, and you helped me search for it. And we found it, after many adventures, propping up Nelson's column. So in the end I got it erected in the fountain's basin in the dead of night, to the deep joy and excitability of the various people who were still up, above all me.

I also had a black boat which represented Charon's Barque, and that day I had sculled on the waters of the fountain, 'unable to hear,' above the plangent plashing, the cries and whistles of the authorities. Eventually they dispatched a humourless personage in rustic green waders who came out of the sun as that poetic saying goes and, clearly taking my innocent voyage personally, tried to tip me out. I clung on, even when my boat was inverted. When that failed, he righted me again and pushed the whole boat backwards over the fountain's parapet, just as in that archetypal scene in the comedy of life when the barrel teeters on the cataract's brink whilst its oblivious occupants woo one another.

There was an evening I spent with my daughters Savannah and Blue who were chained to a sinuous flotilla of bath-tubs which were blocking the Strand. Both escaped arrest on that occasion, but the police later pounced on Savannah, recognising her from the bathtub, and handcuffed her and took her away. There was an evening I slipped away from the demonstration to dinner—not fish—with a fisheries-expert friend. I am working with friends on a project—Ocean Rebellion—to revive the oceans, and who should be on the next table but a government fisheries minister—it sometimes feels we have providence, as well as justice, on our side. Meanwhile the Woodlands Indian restaurant in a nearby back street, and the cafe of the National Gallery, each provided a strange illusion of normality, against a frieze of rebels and police.

Towards the end of the rebellion, Lazer and Savannah took part in a naked protest in the National Portrait Gallery, where with their friend Swan, the three of them lay in radial foetal positions—which reminded me of Bomberg's merry-go-round, or was it Gertler's? Uncertainty, that lost art. And had mock oil poured over them. The National Portrait Gallery launders ludicrously low amounts of money for BP and is allowed in return to display at its entrance BP's enhanced swastika—that robotic chrysanthemum in green and white, a spirograph of malice. Someone wrote to the *Guardian* to say they were sorry they had missed this, a *Three Graces* of our time, the only real art in the show, and had instead only witnessed the incompetent daubs on the walls. It is true that in general, in its twentieth-century collection at least, the NPG seems to be teaching us that beauty does exist as something objective, out in the world itself, and not just in us (unless of course, the world is just in us). They teach this by displaying the absence of it in their collection, which is weird, because to exclude it they must be able to detect it. It is like *Entartete Kunst* (degenerate art), but in reverse.

We had the Writers Rebel reading which I helped put together and at which you read your piece called 'Dear Angelus Novus.' Along with forty eminent and emerging writers. That was poetic—with our audience sitting in the road and being carried away not only *en masse* by literature but one-by-one by the police. It made me think again, as I so often do, of the Eloi and the Morlocks. I suggested that next time it needed to be not the audience but us writers who were carried away, replaced successively by a new writer who would get up in the empty space to read. Margaret Atwood sent an incantation from Canada to be read by Simon McBurney, who I had asked to MC. A.L. Kennedy read Adrian Mitchell's *Tell me Some Lies* adapted to be about the climate emergency, and that was electrifying. I've asked A.L. to read it again at a big press conference we are planning. I should ask if they will let me print it here.

And there were countless meetings and strategy discussions as well—having been hands-on in the April Rebellion, I found myself flying a desk for much of October, as that dream-like saying has it, though my desk was usually the brim of a fountain or the saddle of my bicycle. And I think there was perhaps a confirmation that we needed more tools than just non-violent direct action—tools we have been working up since last summer, to grateful effect, my friends, myself and others within XR—to generate the scale and speed of change that is needed if we are to have a future. NVDA opens the doors and keeps them open (including those of perception)—it is a necessary condition of our success—but we have also to go through the doors and wreak what changes we can inside. And we are finding that by engaging with people on an emotional level, even those compromised and complicit in the carbon-pumping machine (as we all are, whether more or less, let's face it), unexpected changes can suddenly happen.

Anyhow, I don't feel my experience of October was particularly picturesque.

Now tell me, too, what happened to you in October, at the times when we were not together?

And please may we have another Indian meal soon—perhaps at a lovely, deserted place I have been shown on the corner of Cromer Street near the British Library x Roc

On Saturday, 21 December 2019, at 21:41, Susana susanamedina@xr.earth wrote:

Dearest Roc

This is wonderful, so beautiful, thank you. Woohoo!

I'm at a birthday party/book launch (Jan Woolf, *Stormlight*) in a posh hotel in Cricklewood! I'm in the toilet, switched off ... came here to answer some messages ...

Will write tomorrow ...

Tomorrow was planning to finally have a good look at my redrafted 'Trafalgar Sq Rhapsody', so, so good to have your contribution first. Now that I've almost finished my novel, can't wait to finish writing about the October Rebellion, which has been put on hold for so long.

Dinner ... OK ... when would you like to meet?

Must go back to the party ... also, the smell here is getting weird!!! The pervasive fragrance of jasmine air freshener is beginning to unmask unrecognisable layers of smell!

Have a lovely evening. Sx

On Sunday, 22 December 2019, at 06:40, Roc Sandford rocsanford@xr.earth wrote:

Querida Susana,

Writing to you yesterday in your toilet where you had gone to escape the party has made me think of more episodes of the October Rebellion, which I want to send to you. But it also made me think of your 'Rabbit's Foot', the prose poem you have on the wall of your sitting room which I so love. Email me a photograph of it if you can, so I can read it from time to time to laugh and smile, because I have been feeling low and despondent and in pain. Sometimes I understand first-hand how people can find living so painful that to escape it they will even die.

So I like it when Tom Robbins says that in any underground movement (though with our radical transparency, ours is more of an elevated movement) there are both those who are challenging the lethal status quo, and those who are keeping love and joy and beauty alive. I think of Joyce in Trieste, and Auden in Manhattan, each declining the joys of war. And even me in my little boat, sculling on the limpid fountain of Trafalgar Square while all around me police people, soothed by rebels, rage. So I send you a prose poem of mine. It is something of a send-up of Borges, though purple where Borges is spare—purple may be used subversively—because sentimentality is also an emotion, close to the cruelty of which it is the mask. If art is the bottling of emotion for later drinking, then sentimentality, as one of the most dangerous emotions of all, has to be in there, and savoured. Like those Swedish people who eat rotten fish so stinky that they have to be held underwater while being prepared (I ate one once). So in this piece I let my sentimental hair down (it's a wig). I am not sure if you have seen it before, but in case you haven't, here it is. It is called—

TO MILK A UNICORN

Unicorn milk is unbelievable stuff; the highest of the twenty-nine 'angelical liquors' in the flawed enumeration of Averroes. The resolutely bovine get a spiteful buzz in the small of their backs by saying it's no better than cow's milk, and that a unicorn far from being more than a cow, is but a cow, one horn the less. Still, purists compare it with a woman's milk and to the upbeat it gives joy. And, but like most incredible things, it's hard to come by. This is how you must get it. First, go into the woods, the darker the better, though not too dark to see. Clawing wet cobwebs from your face, find a place where curdled fog-streamers are lapped in the inguinal folds of branches, and it smells of mud, fern, Spanish chestnut and honeysuckle. The throstles and the blackbirds sing, but quietly and sadly, and slowly, and at a deeper pitch, so that it sounds not like singing at all, but moaning.

The unicorns at first will look like mist, but glowing brighter than mist. Sometimes their horn is gilded and their mane is blond. This is a trick of the light tumbling as if down a chimney through the forest's needles, dusts, nests and leaves. What you have to do is to look fazed, in trouble, malfunctioning, forlorn. Tangled strands of thick hair blown across your face; some drops of blood tugged from your cheek by a bramble thorn; burrs, sedge and torn nettle-leaves caught both on your crushed-velvet skirt, which is a becoming bottle-green embroidered with wildflowers, and on your flame-coloured jerkin crudely sewn from enormous dead leaves. Something either back to front, upside-down or inside-out to your eyes. And even a fizz and soft sparks from the mussed or felted wiring, fine as hair and wrung by life from a rent in your neck. People who don't know what they are talking about say it is better to be a virgin. They are like those mushroom fanciers who spread self-interested disinformation. Because, no offence intended, soon a unicorn will come, perhaps several.

So—express delight, but in no more than a whimper, because however confidently they cluster round you, they are shy creatures and will soon bolt, even at the thudding of your own heart. Most unicorns have green, grey or brown eyes with vertical pupils and an alert, kindly gleam, not like a target or a cat. But what you want if possible is one with one green and one grey, one grey and one brown, or one brown and one green eye, shaded by thick white lashes. The black ones with dark green eyes are also special. So choose your unicorn, choose the very most best, and take it with you ever deeper into the forest, leading it by the kiss curl that curls down its forehead like a rill, until you find a glade where the sun glares through a sink-hole in the bluish canopy and warms and illuminates plump grass. Which, exactly like your skirt, is studded and spangled with cornflowers, bullrushes and Indian corn, and pansies with smudged eyes, and dawn-coloured crocuses and unripe strawberries; and which looks as if lit from beneath, shining its own lime-green light (with purple patches) on the underside of the unicorn's belly and the frog of your chin. But which gives with a shuddering squelch making brown water trickle around your unicorn's feverish hooves, clumsy and much too big, not canted but drummed, shaded with white fetlock, and the colour of scorched amber. A hollow boom betrays, beneath the saturated grass, the existence of dry rooms filled with twigs and leaves.

Now, curry comb, hoof pick, dandy brush. Fetlock, withers, pastern, rump. There is a Dobbin or even Boxer quality to unicorns, and they will stand still, their legs planted wide and their ears swivelling pleasantly, to be groomed or, later, when you have their trust, ridden. The next bit is the tricky bit. Can you bear to kiss their hot, pink lips, not glazed like our lips, but made of marshmallow skin with stray white hairs, and flobbery. Though mild, they are simple beasts, and sometimes they will think you are giving them sugar and try to nibble off your nose not out of malice but stupidity. Kiss their lips, caress their ears, suck on curly strands of mane, and even tail, out of which if you like you can fashion a living wig and a false moustache, and make them close their eyes by kissing their felted eyelids and blowing along their lashes, whilst all the time (behind your back) hiding a suede bridle inlaid with zinc-plated suns and copper gibbous moons and fitted with a silver-gilt *art-nouveau* Pelham bit adorned with figurines of wood and water nymphs or, if you cannot afford one of those, a bridle made from binder-twine, its reins not plaited but strung, more loosely than a violin bow, with not blond but blonde hair, or black or auburn or grey. The bit must not jingle, nor must your nerves. So, go on caressing the unicorn's ears, but quietly slip the bridle up its face, over the rifled, twisted, barley-sugar-scented horn, clear as a feverish icicle of Coca-Cola, and not frosted but as polished as a lolly ready sucked. Rub its kiss-closed eyes and caressed yet swivelling ears.

Then use your gentle thumb and forefinger in the corners of its lips to open the mouth for the bit. It will shake its head, breathe grassy breath in your face, and pull back, and rear perhaps, but this is a formality. Last but not least, the milk. If you go on caressing your unicorn's ears, it will grow languid and lie itself down in the grass, tuck its hooves with their polished copper shoes under its neat belly, and dreaming it stumbles, will twitch and brace itself in a hypnic jerk. Its breathing slows and you can slip the bridle off (you won't need that anymore) and the unicorn, bridle-less and suddenly resembling a naked woman without her glasses, will toss its head, though without conviction. Then you can blow the conch you have hidden in your clothes, part your own legs, lifting crushed-velvet skirts in ruched swags like a safety curtain to your two hips, one on each side, as milky as unicorn pelt themselves and forming with your milky legs a kind of proscenium arch with a high escutcheon or cartouche. Then, after coating it in your living spit, just as you slick an udder with its own milk, impale yourself so, so slowly, in starts and fits. The sensation for the unicorn is the sweetest in the universe, and it will be yours to take home and keep. But be careful. The point is sharp. Unicorn horn can be really, really sharp. And also brittle. It can easily snap. Or also melt.

On Sunday, 22 December 2019, at 17:39, susanamedina@xr.earth wrote:

Roc

Love your story, thank you for sending it!

The unicorn psychology is so truthful, and the end, impeccable.

When did you write it? Part of a series?

Yesterday I had a long conversation about the unicorn as a symbol for artists with my friend Jo Wonder ... This morning she sent me three drawings of her unicorns in FB (will forward them to you), so started my day with several unicorns!

Love unicorns ... and absurdly, one of my thoughts after the elections was that Scotland would become independent and tragically, English passports will cease to have the unicorn in the coat of arms!!!

You say you've been feeling despondent and in pain ... Is there anything I can do to help? Generally, I'm not feeling that great ... Today, groggy ... had a long sleep.

Above all, thank you gracias for your narrative about the October Rebellion. I can now clearly see how emotional and tough it is being a dad to three rebels, and I am so sorry Blue went through such a hard time when arrested. I have started a submission email of our book to publishers ... What about writing the longest submission email ever? I'll send it to you tomorrow. Sx

On Monday, 23 December 2019, at 21:35, rocsandford@xr.earth wrote:

Querida Susana—

Funny it was a unicorn day for you! I must have tuned in so as to send you my unicorns.

I'm feeling much better. I was really tired but I thought I would send you the email about the October Rebellion before I went to bed and it cheered me up writing it. I've edited it since and made it better. Added a bit about a gorilla lady which I will go back and insert in the text of the dialogue.

Today—lots of XR meetings—about interacting with the media, and with power, and so on.

Tomorrow I'm going up-river to Oxford to stay with my friends Gaspard & Miriam on the banks of the Thames. Maybe back around boxing day.

And then on Saturday back home to Gometra with Savannah and Blue I think. It'll give me time to work on the January trip I am planning to that lair of Moloch, the World Economic Forum in Davos.

Yes, I'd love you to read another of my drafts when you have time. Maybe the novel I had difficulty with which I told you about. It's called *Charm and Strangeness*, which is a phrase from physics as you may know. The heroine is a physicist. Maybe the book about Gometra otherwise—but that's more of a non-fiction book.

Happy Christmas if we don't speak before x

On 23 December 2019, at 22:05, susanamedina@xr.earth wrote:

Dearest Roc

Have been worried about you. What happened?

Yes, I never had a unicorn day before … Astonishing! …

Loved your story. So unexpected.

Good to know you're feeling better.

… Something weird happened this evening. Your unicorn story was on my desk. I'd cut my finger, bandaged it and tiny drops of blood fell on the beginning and the end, framing the story, suddenly making the sharpness of the unicorn horn, real, as if your story was alive. What do you say?

Happy Christmas to Rebel Palace!

… Have been running around like a headless chicken past few days, but have made up a submission letter template to publishers, which speaks a bit about the Rebellion … shall we send it after Xmas …? Here it is:

> Dearest Publisher,

Happy New Year!

Congratulations again on X's glowing reviews and it being shortlisted for the X Prize, and I am sorry about the X Prize strange saga.

It was great to see you at the Global Climate Strike with Poets for the Planet, who are so beautifully active ... So promising to know that over seven million strikers took to the streets. It was orgasmic to scroll through picture after picture of all these cities participating ... Bless Greta Thunberg and all the children!

Above all, apologies for not getting in touch earlier, as I said I would ... As I briefly told you, Roc Sandford and I are writing a dialogue, which includes some fiction pieces and covers all the Extinction Rebellions to date, starting with the great-gamechanger-mesmerising-ever-fabulous-fantastique-amazing Spring Rebellion that changed everything. It is called *Rebel Rebel, An Emergency Dialogue* and we are submitting it to your fascinating publishing house for consideration (we're still to write the last chapter!). Like many rebels, Roc and I became friends during the April Rebellion, and the dialogue also registers the progress in our friendship ... The book can include relevant pictures.

Luckily, *Rebel Rebel, An Emergency Dialogue* got a first puff :):

'My general feeling was yes—it's really interesting. Both as historical snapshot, literary experiment, intellectual exposition, propaganda, didacticism. I also like the collage or 'pastiche' effect of different sorts of writing.' *Roc Sandford.*

During the October Rebellion, Roc was also visiting Roger Hallam (XR co-founder) in prison, and he gave him the following puff:

'I can't see the manuscript because I'm in Wormwood Scrubs prison, but Roc's my man.'

We're still to organise the material for the last chapter. You see, the October Rebellion, which had 'regeneration' as a theme, 'REGEN', we called it, turned out to be traumatic.

As you know, to err is human. *Errare humanum est, perseverare diabolicum!* You might remember the viral video of the police bashing the door of an XR warehouse in Lambeth two days before the Rebellion, on the 5th of October? It was a pre-emptive strike, a bad omen, the start of a long saga of police slights! XR warehouse's door was bashed in order to confiscate, wait: loads of pink pillows!

But worst of all, they confiscated two mobile accessible toilets and showers, wheelchairs, ramps, noise-cancelling headphones for autistic protesters, and solar-powered charging equipment for wheelchairs and scooters. Of course, the seizures were unlawful. And continued throughout: tents, kitchen equipment, laptops, leaflets. The disabled have a long, laudable tradition of fighting against discriminatory treatment, and a small group of members of the XR Disabled Rebels group held a peaceful, non-disruptive protest outside New Scotland Yard with a banner saying 'Give us back our access kit'. They, their personal assistants and carers were arrested, and there were no reasonable adjustments for disabled people in police cells. Imagine the distress, anger and frustration. From day one, the experience was so degrading, even the Metropolitan Police's own disabled advisers lodged a formal complaint. Perversely, we have this situation where peaceful dissent is criminalised, instead of the corporations and politicians that pose much greater threats to our beloved planet. The institutions that are supposed to protect us, prosecute us: according to a report by the independent Network for Police Monitoring (Netpol), the police were accused of abusing their power in more than 500 instances.

Recently, Roc and I met at a delicious vegan café, Paradise Unbakery, in Kensal Rise, and did a post-mortem of the October Rebellion. At some point, he said: 'Trafalgar Square is a traditional place of protest, not enough was being disrupted. The Stock Exchange would have been a better place'. In a way, it would have been a more fitting choice, a top ecological and climate target, given the criminal trade that materialises within its walls. The Bank of England keeps on lending a staggering amount of money to fossil fuel funders. It keeps pumping billions used to fund the destruction of the future. It is intrinsic to the doomsday machine. So, outside the Bank of England would have been good too, and indeed there was an XR Bank Action on the 14th of October, in which Donnachadh McCarthy, who has written at length on the subject, gave a brilliant speech, which he summarised thus: 'If the 10 CEO's in charge of our high street banks teamed up and moved their investments away from fossil fuels and towards sustainable and renewable energy, they could literally change humanity's course for the better and save millions of lives. The UK banks must divest from fossil fuels.'

Both sites would have been appropriate climate and ecological targets, as they're both crime scenes, but I wonder how long we would have lasted there, as those set on perpetuating 'business as usual' and the zombie apocalypse, made sure all the other Rebellion sites were quickly dismantled. Although I kept a diary of sorts, which I am still to edit, I couldn't visit the other sites, so, the diary focuses on Trafalgar Square. This delay in finishing our book is, of course, partly related to the historical omnishambles we are going through, though that is a minor glitch in comparison to the plight of the planet and the existential threat it poses. As you know, it's been quicksands all about us, after the horror of the elections, and Brexit, not to mention the daily revulsion triggered by the Orange Monster and Bolsonaro. And the raging wildfires in Australia. It's been whirlwind after whirlwind, and we all need time to process the profound sadness about how broken the whole thing is.

Also, Roc became diabolically busy, or should I say, heavenly, as he's been working so hard on his halo in several XR groups: XR Catalysers, XR Writers Rebel, Ocean Rebellion, XR Art, the reviving tribal Elders of the West, and recently, XR Political Circle. Of course, with his amazing children, he's always been close to XR Youth too. During the October Rebellion, some days, he'd be doing police liaison, others, talking to fat cats, or talking to the religious leaders. He's been going to Parliament to persuade politicians to act, doing all this work behind-the-scenes. Some of his projects are veiled in secrecy, names, confidential, so I just get abstract scraps of info. He talks to, let's say, a doctor of divinity, and a few weeks later, there's an announcement on *Songs of Praise*—'PRAISE GOD FOR XR.' Or he talks to a prominent businesswoman, and she divests from coal. So, like many full-time rebels, he's subverting the system from within, and busy growing fully functional wings, which is the rational thing to do. And if you are a full-time rebel, writing goes out of the window, at least, while you are at it.

I myself went back to working hard on my novel, a thread of which, by the way, deals with climate change. The end of it is linked to my recent activism. Recently, a delusion hit my neural networks: I thought I had finished it, but nope! ... So, the last chapter of our book gets infinitely postponed. I suppose we are waiting for the right moment, to pick up where we left off. I had asked Roc to send me his thoughts on the October Rebellion. A few days ago, while I was at a party, hiding in a toilet checking my messages, and, admittedly, vaping a bit ... I finally received the requested email from him, followed by a pornographic story called *To Milk a Unicorn*, which he says we should include in the dialogue. God knows! Maybe it isn't all that inappropriate, and has a place there, as a breather from the horror of climate breakdown and ecological collapse. We'll be including it for your consideration.

Well, you get the gist. Enough of excuses for now! We will send you the last chapter and entire manuscript as soon as it is finished.

Looking forward to hearing from you.

Have a lovely day, Roc & Susana x

PS1: Have sent it to an agent, Amanda Anderton (in New York), but they can be so much slower than publishers!!

PS2: I've asked Roc to write, as a coda to the book, about his adventures at the World Economic Forum in Davos which, as you will remember, is also the setting for Mann's *The Magic Mountain*.

PS3: REMEMBER WE ARE TERRORISTS. As I was reading a Monbiot *Guardian* article titled 'If defending life on Earth is extremist, we must own that label' on my iPad, my cat Magic started scratching the PC screen and typed:

?????????????????????????????????????

He couldn't have been more accurate. But at the same time, it's serious:

'Counter-terrorism police in south-east England have listed XR (XR) and the youth climate strikes as forms of 'ideological extremism', alongside terrorists and violent extremist organisations, while the City of London police had listed XR as a 'key threat' in its counter-terrorism assessment. The Counter Terrorism Policing guide to the signs and symbols used by various groups includes: Greenpeace, XR, People for the Ethical Treatment of Animals, CND, the Socialist party, Stop the War and other peaceful green and left organisations.'

Sounds like a sense of humour failure on their part. A dangerous one.

PS4: We might as well include here an overture and short story we are thinking of ending the October Rebellion with. Please scroll down through the blank space:

Goodbye, Pink Cushions & Disability Toilets: The October Rebellion

Do you think the water will forget what we have done. Natalie Diaz

Overture

Cutting and pasting from XR on Twitter a list of items needed, two days before the Rebellion I posted on Facebook:

From Susana Medina, 5 October 2019, 20:52

I hope you're joining the Rebellion from Monday onwards …! The Police have illegally confiscated infrastructure from an XR building in Lambeth. If you can, please take to the Rebellion:

Kitchen equipment – cooking urns and big thermos flasks. Wheelie bins, gazebos and big tents, 250-watt solar panels and 12-volt car batteries, sound equipment and staging, pre-cooked food that's ready to eat, waterproofs, massive umbrellas and hot water bottles.

This raid breached our 'no surprises' policy, though the police retorted that the spraying of litres of red 'blood' onto the Treasury building from a fire engine, two days previously, had come as a surprise to them. That action was truthful, effective and beautiful—one of the best pieces of site-specific political art I have come across. The Treasury is a fundamental cog in the doomsday machine.

The raid was a pre-emptive strike, a bad omen. The Rebellion started Monday, the 7th of October. Unfortunately, I had to teach a new course at the Open University, which began this very same day, but I'd decided I'd dash out to Trafalgar Square and the other sites as much as possible and help with whatever I could. In any case, I would be there as a Writer in Residence. Trafalgar Square, the main site, was named Burning Earth. The weather forecast was heavy rain. I'd try to juggle time, and wear groovy clothes to defuse low morale. It was going to be a Wet Rebellion. I told Roc. He was there first thing in the morning, and messaged:

> Brought black umbrella and waterproof trousers. All quiet here on Traf Sq except for traffic and drumming, and blue lighters going through to other sites. It's early, it's not full, but it will be.

I joined him soon afterwards, with my XR flag and an orange bag for life filled with a wok, biscuits and spices. Every time I went to the square, I did outreach on the tube, and told those who said they'd come to previous rebellions: 'XR is not just for Xmas!' While giving out XR leaflets on the train, I had engaging conversations with commuters. The most memorable one was with an alien-looking beautiful creature, a young black Swedish man with extraordinary turquoise eyes, undoubtedly a sexual angel, who told me he read *The Uninhabitable Earth* when it first came out and was so terrified he instantly switched to renewable energy, gave up red meat, gratuitous consumption and flights. That day I began a story about the October Rebellion.

Trafalgar Sq Rhapsody

To Iggy Fox

We are nature. We are science. We turn grief into action. We protest and we sing and we play and we dance. We do so for life. We are mourning the earth. We are mourning us. We are re-inventing the city. We are the grief-stricken carnival spirit that marks XR, making it a bittersweet joy to walk into a transfigured Trafalgar Sq, XR flags, with their bright colours and bold graphic design, flying high in the air, all roads freshly blocked, the large traffic circle replaced by exuberance.
  Trafalgar Square is about to become a playground.
  Rebels, tourists and the world press snap away.
  The bronze statues of lions proudly wear their large XR medallions.
  There is no traffic soundtrack, but the traffic lights beam their usual colours.

The stench of burnt petrol will fade away.
The smog will vanish.
The square will disown concrete.

We are sorry. We have a sacred duty to rebel. We chant, disrupt carbon emissions and pray for sanity. Our presence translates the trauma of omnicide. Our utopian smiles, adrenaline and bonhomie pervade the air, transforming the asphalt into a transcendent place of sorrow, laughter and hope. Gyrating in front of a THIS IS AN EMERGENCY fuchsia banner which blocks a street, here are the astonishing hula-hoop rebels, a group of delicious young women with hula-hoops ceaselessly spinning around their arms a tale of defiance. Diagonally blocking Whitehall, black humour takes the shape of a fantastically ghoulish hearse with floral tributes for the final journey, OUR FUTURE written along the black ribbon which rests on the coffin, the XR symbol centred on its back, while two rebel chauffeurs are locked to the steering wheel, ready for the planet's funeral. In yellow vests and flat peak caps, the police guard the funerary ceremony, arms crossed, legs wide apart, perhaps wondering whether play might be the highest form of revolt. The samba magic begins to bind us in rhythm. It features a gutsy old lady rebel in a wheelchair drumming away, joyfully, furiously, her XR drum.

Here is the future. It transforms autumn into spring. It playfully bids adieu to a culture of death. A new vision of human nature is out on the streets, a ritual to give form to grief. Here, in the soon-to-be-filled-square, are the piles of kitchen utensils and food brought by all of us, to make up for the police seizures. Here is charming Roc with his beguiling smile, as a dad of mighty rebels, artist and writer, dressed smartly for his police liaison role. Here is radiant white-haired Lorna by the fountain, her luminous eyes focused on her mobile, as she coordinates legal support for the imminent arrests. Blocking the asphalt from side to side, lock-ons will keep multiplying on all the roads. Surrounded by police in yellow vests, it is mostly elderly conscientious protectors lying on the road locked-on, arms spread out, holding hands, a human chain of veteran activists: 'I am willing to be arrested', their placards say. Dutifully visiting them, here is the Red Brigade, a large crimson splash of mourning humans with faces painted white, and black tears, a solemn presence, sorrowful and soothing at once.

I will be arrested in a few days' time, when I finish the mountain of work. Like so many rebels, I will have to organise my own arrest. I am also caring for my mother. I will take her to my brother's flat. I will be available for arrest from Thursday onwards.

I now capture moments of hope in action, the thing with feathers that won't ever take 'no' for an answer. At the centre of it all, an unforgettable three-and-a-half feet tall rebel with a circled hourglass painted on her cheek, over her head a light pink handkerchief with a bee block-printed at the front, and an XR scarf over an orange duffel coat.

With startingly large eyes, she's screaming and screaming at the police.

Frowning, always on the verge of crying, she yells:

'Leave my mummy alone!'

'Don't touch her!'

The police are trying to arrest some rebel mothers blocking the road, their faces contorted. Her rebel mother is sitting on the road, a baby on her lap. Most fathers and mothers can only but be rebels. The rebel mothers stay put.

Arms wide apart, the little rebel girl stands in front of her mum.

'There is a plague in the sky. And in the earth. And in the seas.'

Astonished, rebels and bystanders watch the feisty little rebel girl. Black fringe, black eyes, pale complexion, three-and-a-half feet tall, hourglass on her cheek, head, chest. How old is she? Five? She is the future of the planet, if we cherish it enough to protect it. One day, she could have grey hair and laughter lines, if we care for her future. Discombobulated, a policeman, clasped hands with interlocked fingers, crouches next to her. He is forcing himself back, exercising some sort of self-restraint, his body language conveying great anxiety and frustration. He watches her speechless, obviously thinking: 'Things are going really badly.' The only way he can talk to the little rebel girl is by crouching next to her. All the police are crouching around her, so she is just a bit taller than them. The little rebel girl commandeers the situation. The world is her oyster, but the planet is dying. She's one of the many Gretas who won't stop screaming until we all listen. Suddenly, she's all the Gretas, whatever their age and gender, as well as all the different names all the Gretas have. The little feisty girl has the power.

A helicopter soon starts circling the sky above the square.

'My mummy's protesting for the common good!' the little rebel girl yells.

The crouching policeman looks as if gripped by a moral dilemma, words caught in his throat. He rests his hand on his heart. A policewoman, pursed lips, plump hands, thumbs tucked under her fingers, requests the rebels to get up and leave the square. 'Sit down, sweetheart,' the rebel father says, but the little rebel girl isn't finished with her intervention.

Always on the verge of crying, pointing her forefinger at the policewoman, the little rebel girl yells:

'We are doing this for your children

We are the children who know what you're doing

We want to live

We want the birds and the trees and the sky to live

And the elephants, butterflies, penguins and the monkeys, the pandas and the zebras

And the seas, rivers, the fishes, turtles, hippos, giraffes, rhinos and the tigers, lions and the bumblebees and the insects. Don't you get it?'

The little rebel girl bursts into tears.

Disarmed, the police leave.

The rebel parents hug and kiss their daughter.

With its hideous roar, the helicopter continues to circle the sky.

There is everyday heroism, and everyday villainy.

We are zing, pluck, zest, vim. We protest and we sing and we play and we dance. Drumming binds us. There are no XR boats this time. We are the boat. A scaffolding tower is quickly conjured up in front of Waterstones. At its top, lovely Fox waves a large magenta XR flag with a skull at its centre, and symbols of life pushed to its edges. The scaffolding tower becomes an XR citadel, as young rebels glued to it, well-known beloved faces, start giving passionate speeches. There is clapping and sing-alongs.

Mooney, Blue, Fox with his red Rapunzel hair.

I saw Fox a couple of days before, at the Rebel Palace, sitting on a white sofa, felt pen in hand, focusing on a large map spread out on the floor. I sat next to him, trying to make sense of the map. 'If you look at this map, I'll have to kill you.' It was the map of the Rebellion. When I left the room, I whispered: 'Gracias for sparing my life!'

I crane my neck to look at Mooney, Blue, Fox with his red Rapunzel hair.

I read it in the papers: this time the police will make use of a specialised team who use the latest technology to quickly unglue rebels.

Darkness descends, it has the face of the specialised team, up on the scaffolding tower.

It's the first day, it's only 3 o'clock and the arrests begin.
It is profoundly upsetting.
Because to be arrested is wrong, and to be arrested is vital.
I take pictures of Rapunzel's red hair, hanging from the metal bars of the scaffolding tower as he's handcuffed. It's as if he had let down his long red braid so that we could all climb up to them, back to the scaffolding tower. I take pictures of him lying down, waving an #ActNow flag, trying to make it visible while he's being arrested.
There are sing-alongs:
Power to the People
Cos the people got the power
Tell me can you hear it
Getting stronger by the hour
Power!
People!
People!
Power!

And while we sing, I see Fox's red Rapunzel hair blowing with the wind, video camera in hand, in a flashback to May day, the day of the national declaration of an Environment and Climate Emergency. It was a lovely video moment, after the Carnival of Chaos organised outside the Brazilian Embassy to protest Bolsonaro's vicious destruction of the Amazon. We were ecstatic. We'd moved back into Trafalgar Square with the Red Brigade, to the beat of samba magic. Fox was filming, he was smiling, and smiling I hugged him and started screaming 'We won! We won, ha, ha!' while whirling around with him, and saying 'Give us a kiss!' while he's saying: 'We haven't won, yet!' And he is movement. His red Rapunzel hair blows in the air, his red Rapunzel hair gathers everyone up.

And the arrests continue. And we paint the streets. We protest in the morning, in the afternoon, in the evening, and at night. We protest and we sing and we play and we dance.

XR Youth rebels sit on top of the scaffolding, their legs dangling in the air. One by one, they will be arrested. Writers Rebel arrive, smiles sliding across their faces: Monique, James, Toby, Cath, Roc. Young pretty things hand out paper bags with 'Rebels with a Cause' hand-written on them: inside, a healthy sandwich, a granola bar, an apple. Beautifully tribal, yellow eye-shadow Mooney gives a passionate speech. The emotional rollercoaster begins. It will intensify. Courageous, rosy-cheeked, blue-eyed Blue is crying. Intelligent tears pool under her glasses, while the legal observers take note of the police actions. There are more arrests and more loud cheers. There are sing-a-longs, arrests and loud cheers. A tall woman wearing a First World War gas mask hangs around the police van, adding to the dystopian mood. Blue is next. The air starts turning sullen. And I must go, I have to work.

On my way to the tube, passing the multi-coloured community of tents where rebels will sleep night after night, I see all the teamwork and transformative care behind every action, reaction and idea. I see all the hours behind the carnival spirit and the behind-the-scenes work. Tonight, there'll be hot water bottles, for those camping through the liquid nights. Tomorrow, waiting for the arrestables, there'll be arrestee support, first aid, a hug and a mug of hot chocolate. Kindness is catching. On the tube railing, there is a large yellow banner that reads in black bold typeface: EMPATHY.

The hourglass is ubiquitous, on flags, clothes, drums, sculptures. Decorated with Stop Ecocide placards, high-flying XR flags and stickers, the lock-on towers keep on growing, playful fortresses where rebels glue themselves with superglue. The vibrancy is palpable. Familiar faces rebel as if their lives depended on it, because their lives are also the lives of others, including all life on earth, present and future. Here is cheeky Savannah, wearing her beautiful torn clothes. Here is Clarissa, a big mama rebel in pink waterproofs, who turns away when she sees I'm about to take a picture of her. 'How are you?' I say. 'Not good!' ... 'How come?' 'The police confiscated £1000 worth of kitchen equipment ... and now they're saying they've lost it!'

Her face is full of despair.

She strides on.

We'll be fighting against this impulse to destroy. And demoralise. You would think the natural instinct is to preserve life, but it seems to run counter to those worshipping big profit. In the square, renamed 'Burning Earth', there are series of large paper tombstones IN MEMORIAM to murdered activists. Reading their names and the epitaphs, the soul stops, and weeps. The cult of profit is the cult of death.

We protest in the morning, in the afternoon, in the evening, and at night. We protest and we sing and we play and we dance. Today there'll be rebels, parents, lovers and friends waiting outside police stations to welcome the release of arrestables. Heaven opens upon us, and hundreds of rebels run for shelter to the gazebos, but alas, there aren't enough of them, as they've been confiscated. Torrential rain will punctuate the Rebellion. We stretch tarpaulin and plastic sheets over bare structures, and hold them with cable ties. Beautifully tribal, yellow eye-shadow Mooney and I make a good team. Even with the improvised gazebos, we are packed like sardines, wet, bewildered. Fortunately, glued people lying on the tarmac have umbrellas, though the liquid streets are unforgiving.

We are all crew. We are the boat that rocks the boat. We look after each other and feed each other. An old rebel shivering next to me tells me the police have been using intimidation tactics in the past 48 hours. 'Stop and search,' he says. 'You see, grief is subversive. Grief is not a negotiation with death; it is a courageous love letter to life.'

Reluctant daleks follow instructions to violate the peaceful joyous atmosphere, to destroy, to suck our spirit. They do so in front of large heart flags that read: 'Humility, Empathy, Frugality.' When the rain subsides, the square quickly fills up again. A man with a gigantic inflatable dinosaur floating on a pole with a 'Business As Usual' placard parades around Nelson's Column speaking out with a megaphone: 'Where is the sense of urgency? Climate change is killing us, a quarter million a year. A quarter million, a figure that will increase annually. Deadly heatwaves are killing us. Death by overheating will increase. Extreme weather is killing us, but there are no climate change death certificates, oh no. 60 per cent of natural wildlife has been destroyed, but bulldozing, deforestation and poisoning continues, oh yes.' A rebel lady with the blue planet painted on her cheek nods: 'We are governed by utter fuckweasels setting fire to the present and the future.' The plywood playful lock-on towers, made of stacked modules with circular holes to accommodate glued-on arms, begin to look like citadels. Here is writer Sue, a strong vibrant presence in all the rebellions. With her bald head, large peace symbol earrings, relentless energy and elastic smile, she's on a mission to be arrested as many times as possible, and it's always, oh, so good seeing her doing what she must do. We exchange smiles. Sadly, I must go home, and work. As I walk to the station, a hundred-year-old man gets carted away by the police, clapped by a multitude of rebels.

We rise. We rise up. A new day. All over social media, a non-binary giant pink octopus, named Jeanne-Luc, eyes made of upside-down blue basins with the XR symbol painted on, is roaming the streets of Whitehall. There are surreal images of the police kettling and carrying an arrested pink octopus! Like many rebels, every day, when I can, I grab food for the kitchen tent and my XR flag and rush to the square for as long as I can, then back to work. I wonder how many rebels are coming and going, coming and going. I rush to the square and walk lightly around. Jeanne-Luc, the pink octopus is still there, enjoyed by children and adults alike. In the yoga tent, gracious rebels stretch slowly, their choreographed movements speaking about how human health and planetary health are woven into each other. By the fountain, there are many rebel mothers with their babies in buggies or holding them in their arms. It is sunny. And today is their day: a mass nurse-in.

There are only a few trees at the square. There is laughter, and invisible tears, tension and carnival spirit. Soon, laughter and joyous spirit begin to crack: the police have begun to slash tents with scissors. They are violently removing tents. A distressed pregnant woman holds a torn piece of tent. A couple from Animal Rebellion who camped overnight tell me: 'This morning they've confiscated our laptops, food, tents. They're destroying personal property before inventorying it. They just indiscriminately chuck everything in the rubbish lorry. They've even confiscated little skeleton turtles we made!'

'Drop out of the fairy tale,' they say.

But it ain't exactly a fairy tale. It's a new story implored by science, a cautionary tale with gruesome fairy-tale elements and a vision: we'd like a happy ending.

Is that a bird singing?

The enemies of life are in power, turning the planet into a warmer and wetter horror show. To be human is to care. We subvert and we jam, while eight-metre artificial silk flags which speak of the burning planet and melting icebergs tremble in the air. At Waterstones' cafeteria, Liz, Chloe, Roc and I share banner and flag materials to put together at home, for Writers Rebel's famous 40 Top Writers Marathon. We protest and we sing and we play and we dance, while parents rush around checking on their teenage children, to guard them on lock-on, or to be with them when they're arrested. A snaking flotilla of bathtubs painted purple, yellow, green, maroon springs up near the bookshop: inside them, locked-on XR Youth rebels. We protest in the morning, in the afternoon, in the evening, and at night.

We make waves out of vibrancy and spunk. We sleep in tents, in the liquid square, enduring liquid nights. The rain hasn't deterred Ex Met Detective John Curran from gluing himself to the pavement at an XR protest at City Airport. He has now been arrested. Over a thousand rebels have been arrested. The good news is it is all over the news.

In the rain-soaked square, slashed tents: this is what democracy looks like.

  The rain subsides. A diabolical mammoth cherry picker presides over the Waterstones side of the square, now seething with lines and lines of police in black, in yellow, their old-fashioned mobile phones held on their chests. It would be beautiful if some of them joined our protest in solidarity, but their body language says *Bestellungen sind Bestellungen*, orders are orders. It also says: Judge those who Pull the Strings. The doomsday machine has birthed a monstrous cherry picker that will dismantle a lock-on tower and allow to unglue locked-on rebels. We gasp, we frown in anguish, tight lips. We keep da faith. We will hold on against the odds. The beautiful flotilla of painted bathtubs is in a pile together with sleeping bags, banners, placards, all ready to be vanished into the rubbish lorry. The carnival of resistance continues: rebels parade large skeletons of fish, birds, humans at the end of long poles, while in Whitehall, strong, fit men dressed as kangaroos leaping on stilts dazzle everyone, except for a nervous dog.

  We risk our freedom, some of us sleep in slashed tents in the liquid nights. At dusk, surrounded by the XR police liaison team with their baby blue waistcoats, Roc liaises with the police about the Writers Rebel event, making sure no writers at the event tomorrow will be arrested, Blue, his sweet rebel daughter, shadowing him. It is getting late. Almost dinner time. It is always a joy to see the yellow and green chant-Hare-Krishna-and-be-happy bicycle cart, to smell the kindness as they hand out free vegetarian warm meals to the long queue of rebels.

We wave our new flags and brandish words that speak of untold suffering and our shared humanity. We writers want to unwrite earth's fate, edit it out, rewrite it. The ever-helpful police have seized our sound system and the stage, but we will persevere in our being. Here comes the stage, and the speakers. Here comes Jessica, with her XR-customised pink coat, carrying a microphone. We read out loud on the ravages of fire, flooding, and the new deserts. We read out loud on the war on nature and the trail of destruction the doomsday machine leaves behind. We grieve the victims of climate change and the fact that we are all fucked. We sing and we weep invisible tears and we listen and we read. It is the amazing Writers Rebel 40 UK Writers event, with its brave audience sitting on the floor. We are thrilled by Margaret's passionate words about this time capsule found on the dead planet. We are electrified by Alice's fiery 'tell me lies about climate change'.

Lies, lies, lies, which will continue throughout next year.

The criminal lack of action will continue.

We listen, frowning in anger. We ask for arrestables. We'll soon have to brave the weather. As night falls, the Red Brigade, a tragic reminder of the blood shared by all species, pay us homage with their sacred presence. On stage, Simon bows to these unforgettable emissaries of spirituality. The daring audience open their umbrellas and stay put. Torrential rain cascades down, and drenched, we scatter and decamp under the arcades, by Waterstones. We read out loud and we shiver and we listen, while arrests continue in the rain. We read out loud and we weep invisible tears.

At the end of the liquid odyssey, we celebrate defying the odds.

Ravenous, we eat delicious food from the five-star rebel kitchen tent. The fountain is illuminated. The cold night blurs the lights around their edges, the wet asphalt reflects uncertain shadows. Here is Roc looking for his black pyramid. Here is Hugo, a guerrilla gardening rebel who tells me he recently lost his mother, and he sobs, and we hug for an eternal instant. Samba magic transforms the moment and we part. Here is a lock-on citadel where rebels hope to be soon arrested. Here is Roc again. I join in the search for his walk-in pyramid, a conical black costume made from wood with a slit at eye level and a lockable door that allows you to hide inside, to protect yourself from the police. Austere and absurd, it's like an armour, something medieval and monty-pythonesque about it. We look for it in the large piles of seized equipment behind metal fences. We look and we look. We find it and we play.

We reclaim the streets. We cycle. We have to work. We give our time. We are at the square. We take time off to regenerate. We share and re-tweet. There is comedy. And there is tragedy. On social media there are pictures of the police arresting a man dressed up as broccoli, though Mr. Broccoli looks fantastic, and as yet, there are no laws against dressing up as a superpower vegetable. But as a prelude of what's to come, there are also shocking pictures of an upside-down wheelchair thrown on a slashed gazebo by the rubbish lorry.

The square welcomes the Citizen's Assembly.

Here is George, the journalist, in Whitehall. He has publicised with great fanfare his arrest, declaring: 'We have only one strength, our vulnerability.' And with a gleeful smile, he is now carried away from

Whitehall by four policemen, as XR flags fly high in the blue sky. There is clapping, there is chanting. Governments know the truth about the climate and ecological emergency, but most of them are there to protect the doomsday machine. To remind us, here is a group of interfaith rebels with a choir from XR Christian Climate Action. As if they were the new commandments, melodiously they sing XR's demands:

Tell the truth: Government must tell the truth by declaring a climate and ecological emergency, working with other institutions to communicate the urgency for change; Act Now: Government must act now to halt biodiversity loss and reduce greenhouse gas emissions to net zero by 2025; Beyond Politics: Government must create and be led by the decisions of a Citizens' Assembly on climate and ecological justice.

We are gutted, we are outraged: the planet is dying and civil liberties are under threat.

While some of us sleep, others are arrested. While some of us rest, the Metropolitan Police have issued a draconian Section 14 order, banning any assembly linked to XR in the capital. It's 9:00 pm. It's raining. The blaring sirens seize the wet square. The police are breaking up the camp, the last rebels remove their drenched tents, while a helicopter circles the night with its chopping menace.

The liquid square is empty: it is now a crime for rebels to be here.

The circle of traffic returns.

I won't be arrested, as planned.

We backfill the square, bathed in luminous light. It's full house, a multitude of XR flags waiving against the blue sky. Rebels keep on coming, while rebel children read or draw in the gentle autumn sun warming the afternoon, sitting on the steps below the National Gallery. At the top of the steps, the speakers are getting ready. Here is Rupert, now looking tense, now looking forward to the future, while holding a placard that says: 'Reflect, Rebel, Relinquish.' A thousand cameras snap away, documenting our defiance of the ban. We are grit, but we are also spoken by anger, disappointment, perplexity, sadness. We have been ripped apart, and put back together in an awkward way. At the top of the steps, we unfurl a large red banner with writing in white lower-case letters:

The utter incredibleness of existence; of life. Billions of years of ever-refining complexity, diversity, intricacy, beauty. We are just one species amongst millions, and this we knowingly dismantle. Where is our sense of awe, of wonder, of humility?

Passionate speeches begin, trailed by incantatory chanting: we are responsible, another world is possible. Soon, children take centre stage: A fiery eight-year-old blond rebel wearing an orange miniskirt and a furry leopard jacket bravely addresses over a thousand rebels: 'There is only one world. No Planet. B. Only use plastic if you really need it!' We grin and we clap. We will not be silenced. Change is now. Change happens with never-ending action. Another little rebel girl, an XR sticker on her short black coat, takes hold of the microphone: 'If you want to survive ...'

    Mid-sentence, as if overcome by the enormity of her first words, she looks away and turns to one side. A prolonged silence fills up the square. The silence screams. We smooth out the silence with soothing chanting. The law will be with us. We will win the landmark case against the police. We patiently wait to be arrested, but there are no arrests. The police are there, yellow vests, arms crossed. Above all, we won't lose hope, while being aware that hope is not a strategy. Our self-renewing resolve erases the uncertain road ahead. We will do action after action after action. The samba magic returns. We protest and we sing and we play and we dance. We re-imagine the world. Dear lost people, we are one of the maps.

January 2020: The Tragic Mountain, or The Four Planes of Davos

> His face is turned toward the past. Where we perceive a chain of events, he sees one single catastrophe which keeps piling wreckage upon wreckage and hurls it in front of his feet. The angel would like to stay, awaken the dead, and make whole what has been smashed. But a storm is blowing from Paradise; it has got caught in his wings with such violence that the angel can no longer close them. The storm irresistibly propels him into the future to which his back his turned, while the pile of debris before him grows skyward. The storm is what we call progress. *Walter Benjamin*

Dark Wood

Dear Susana,

You've asked me to write to you about coming to Davos.

Well, I usually travel looking for a home-to-be. But this time I travelled to save one, the only one I'll ever get, this weird, marbled bubble whirling through the manifold with trees and people clinging to it.

As you know, I have always felt XR's brand of peaceful protest, while a necessary condition, to be an insufficient one for averting our fate, and that dialogue with the powerful was both necessary and insufficient too.

Though Davos is only a village, once a year, for this sole week in January, it is also the stage on which is played a drama whose subtext is the end of the world. Moloch receives you in the comfort of his lair. What could be more interesting than that? Besides, this drama not only represents the world's fate, but *is* it—in the sense that there are people here who, to a Wagnerian soundtrack, are pushing on the levers of Apocalypse as I speak.

As Dracula might have it, the stakes couldn't be higher.

And—the fate of the world is the fate of the self-conscious universe, if we are the only ones fitted to reflect it. If this planet is just what it looks like, an eyeball floating in space.

So, a few thousand people with all the power in the universe—a tiny Greta, feeling ill, with whom you stroll down the village street; a swelling, oddly coloured Trump, dropped in like a spiteful demiurge by chopper. You share the tinkling urinals, alone, with an ex security council head of state, who had personally shaken the geopolitical foundations of the world-order, whilst their detail, mouths to wrists, wait politely outside. The illusion, at Davos, is that you know all these people and, good or bad, angelic or horrific, they live in your village. The television screen dissolves like a looking glass, and Alice mingles with the people on the news.

And even Alice, it turns out, has power—more than she knows. Some have a deterministic view of history—that it will do its thing whatever we do, and like someone driving a train, we can't choose where it goes only, at most, how fast. For me history is more capricious. We think of its structure as impersonal, but it is humans with power in the widest sense, including the power of the unfortunate, the beautiful, the young—Salomé danced with Herod's power—with all our greed, idiocy, compassion, who invite history to come to pass. I am with Akhmatova on this and against Tolstoy and Marx. History shares in our free will. Kantian free will, even, or quantum—the imperative, usually denied, to override our motives and to be rational and unpartisan.

I'm comfortable believing in such freedom, against all evidence, because either I am right, or I didn't have a choice—this is to wake from the unpleasantly calculating nightmare of Pascal's wager. Likewise, with history—if I fail in helping to thwart its suicide, for deterministic reasons at least, rather than just personal feebleness, then it wasn't possible anyway.

The trouble is, that's a lot of humans with power Alice must onboard if restoring the freedom of history is her project—lest her particular onboarded humans are off-boarded by the rest, and the placid grinding of life itself by the powerful should resume.

Beforehand, I hadn't been convinced there was any point in coming here. Either Davos would turn out to be something like the *Wizard of Oz*—someone behind a curtain, quite disappointing, but with a booming voice (i.e. the propaganda media). Or even a dalek—an atrophied lizard-thing inside an infernal engine which, as I noted gravely when taken to our local cinema as a child to see what I mistook for a newsreel, is confined to tarmac and couldn't chase Doctor Who off-piste.

Or else, I feared, if it turned out there *was* still power residing in Davos, we as XR would be like hitch-hikers on a wet motorway, turning our sodden heads to watch the limos pass.

It was, it turned out, not like that—some of the limos stopped to pick us up. And even, sitting on their laps as it were, let us think we drove. Because, as we learned from countless conversations, the system is crumbling from inside, and some of the people within it, but ever more, understand that the game is up, and that for love of their families, the emissions and extinctions must stop. Unless that is just their own form of sweet-talk, and my own form of denial. Unless we were just being pumped for intel and consolation all along.

Intel doubtless included the news I had brought two books—Mann's *The Magic Mountain*, translated by Lowe-Porter, and Kafka's *The Castle*, translated by Willa and Edwin Muir. I'd read both before. Like this very email I'm sending you now, *The Magic Mountain* is set in Davos.

> He looked out. The train wound in curves along the narrow pass; he could see the front carriages and the labouring engine vomiting great masses of brown, black, and greenish smoke, that floated away. Water roared in the abysses on the right; on the left, among rocks, dark fir-trees aspired toward a stone-grey sky.

The earth has spun its candy-floss around the sun a hundred times and has sparkled with the smoked glitter of two world wars since. But I, reading those words, had caught the same train.

I didn't have the heart to read more as, after changing like Mann's hero Hans at Landquart, we wound upwards beside single-minded torrents, amongst chilly forests and under vain crags. I wanted only to look out the window. There were plants rocking in our slipstream. And cuttings walled in cliff. But then the plants were replaced by banks of snow and the cliffs by icicles. Sometimes I would see the foggy road, also climbing, its tranquilised curves and cambers masking an efficient horror, and its regular convoys of black limos rattling—like the ghosts of wilful toddlers who are never now to be— their snow-chains, with their wipers swishing and their headlamps lit.

All driving, I reflected, is drunk driving. Petrol is a psycho-active drug which gladdens then poisons the spirit. The car is just the glass we use to drink it.

As a teenager I had loved *The Magic Mountain*. Turning its pages again, as darkness fell and I could no longer see anything in the carriage window but myself, I liked a passage of Walter Benjamin's, quoted in the introduction, enough to copy it down—

> A generation that had gone to school in horse-drawn street-cars now stood under open sky in a landscape in which nothing remained unchanged but the clouds, and below them, in a force-field crossed by devastating currents and explosions, stood the tiny, fragile, human body.

Now, of course, even the clouds are changed and the tiny, fragile, human body is facing ever more devastating horrors. To which the horrors of the last century will be but a feeble warm-up—just as the horror of the migrants and plutocrats freezing to death in their cork life-vests whilst the Titanic rocketed towards the seabed beneath their dangling feet, carrying with it their luggage, were feeble warm-ups for the Great War, the Soviet Terror, the Holocaust. We are just like children whose eyes are covered at the scary bits. This, now, here, the time we are living, is a scary bit, the scariest there's ever been and—our eyes are covered! We could be screaming—but instead we recline in temporarily cosy denial in the corner seat of a railway carriage, flipping the brittle pages of a second-hand *Magic Mountain*, acquired in Zurich.

Purgatorio

Unlike Mann's Hans I got off at Schiers, a few stops before Davos, looking for Swiss XR who, as part of *Snow Rebellion*, had told me they would camp for the night there. Snow Rebellion had been trudging through the momentous landscape, some dressed as scorched koalas, towards the out-of-joint feast high above.

There is something alarming about getting off a hot train, which you have made your temporary home, into the frozen night of a small, darkened village. But in the icy star-pricked night, I eventually found them clustered around a brazier, feeding on chocolate mousse.

The koalas felt slightly crazed. Understandably, given their eucalypt woodlands were currently on fire and their fur was smoking. Cuddly fellow-koalas were dying in agony in their millions—writhing, squirming, dropping suddenly from charred trees like flaming fruit and landing with sizzling thuds. The koala-rebels at Schiers were, like me, seeking how to pierce denial, complacency, the moral idiocy that we all share—and they had dressed as singed koalas to bring the plight of the sizzling home to its seat in the jamboree of the world economic system. They too, like me and my XR Catalyser friends, were here to be ghosts at this feast.

Leaving them at last, moved by their resolve, I wandered around in the dark for a while, lost in the suburbs of what itself was but a snowy village, unable to locate even the railway tracks, and finding the station only when, on the rim of panic, led there by a friendly villager.

It was an illusion of parallax but by morning the singed koalas who, as they presented themselves to the eye of my wakening mind, had resumed their dogged ascent towards that abyss of horror represented by Davos—and by horror I don't mean the people here, so much as our field-effect on human suffering—these dogged and brave koalas appeared to be marching in place, like a looped cartoon. It was so hot in the imagined snows through which they plodded that they had flopped back their koala-hoods, revealing perspiring human heads with plastered hair.

It is no accident that writing, too, as you and I know, is also a marching in place. How ever many words you write, you still look up and find that you are lying in the same bed or sitting at the same café table as when you started, the road before you, paved with glittering words, perhaps still longer than before.

Inferno

It was late when my train finally clanked into Davos Dorf aka Gehenna and, with a pointed shriek, stopped. The station was deep in snow. Around it in the darkness were the lights of the village.

Arriving here I had felt the same confusion as Mann's Hans, which was that however much I tried to memorise the name of the station I was supposed to alight at, I couldn't—was it Davos Dorf or Davos Platz? There is something disordered, even mobile, about a place you have never been. But like Hans, I too had a friend awaiting me. There he was, and I climbed down. After the train shrieked out, I saw that planks had been laid between the rails to make a wooden path across the railway. And there was a bridge, too, across the frozen river. The roads, I found, were made of solid ice. I remembered Kafka's K. arriving at the scene of his coming struggle—

> The Castle hill was hidden, veiled in mist and darkness, nor was there even a glimmer of light to show that a castle was there. On the wooden bridge leading from the main road to the village, K stood for a long time gazing into the illusory emptiness above him.

> Then he went to find quarters for the night.

My friend led me to the immense white marquee, carpeted in navy, warmed by noisy industrial blow-heaters, and filled like an airport check-in with serpentine queues, at which I was to collect my biometric ID badge. It felt like one of those tacky trade fairs held in great exhibition centres—the *Boat Show*, the *Caravan and Camping Show*, the *Ideal Home Exhibition*. Only, what was displayed here for sale was the ultimately fungible commodity, power itself. All the horse-trading takes place in the five *belle époque* hotels. Given the abnormal density of heads of state, multinational CEOs, finance ministers and billionaires, these have airport-style security at their gates and can only be entered with such a badge. Once it was issued, on a fine yellow lanyard, my friend led me through snows to the very Swiss flat, suffocatingly clean and hot, which his aunt, our lead-Virgil, had found for me and the six rebel friends who were still on their way.

Exhausted though I was, I stayed up late reading Kafka. Unlike Joseph K.

of Kafka's *The Trial*, the K. of *The Castle* will not simply argue against the judgment. K. challenges the right to judge and would, if he could only get there, take his struggle inside the citadel of authority, to the very bedrooms of his judges.

My plight was similar, only I had to get not into bedrooms, but minds. If it really were impossible to avert the disaster and wean the world off fossil fuels, then XR would be a powerful anaesthetic, taken to blunt the pain of unavoidable doom. But it *cannot* be impossible, because the doom can't be accepted—the end of history, literature, music, children, babies, animals, birds—cannot *be*—cannot even be *risked*—our wills must rise to the occasion of declining this because all along, as it turns out, this has been what they were for. To refuse!

'What must be done, sir, will be done,' said Dr Johnson to Boswell.

Kleist's hero, Michael Kohlhaas, used his own body to jam the grinding-machine. With the integrity of a Talleyrand and the cunning of an Odysseus he made himself ungrindable. Time will tell whether it is possible, in our case, to jam the life-grinder, but time will never tell that it is impossible because before knowing that, we'll be gone—and so we too must go on offering ourselves up as ungrindables, perhaps only to be ground. As Pasternak puts it, 'There isn't any point in dying without a struggle, like sheep.'

So, like Kohlhaas, K. doesn't passively accept the authority of the court and simply oppose its judgement, he actually goes after it and challenges its existence. And perhaps this reflects a change in me too—a reluctance to accept the fate being dished up for us, but a decision to decline it. I refuse.

To flourish the XR flag inside the citadel, the carbon castle, was our project. And I found that, as K. was told in *The Castle*, a word, a glance, a sign of trust sometimes moved the levers of power. We were to have many meetings with those with their hands on these and sometimes, after such meetings, you heard, if only in your imagination, the subtle creaking of levers being pushed.

Despite the snows, the following morning was hot. Weather-wise, we were in the fifth season—that of derangement and evil—it was the alluring but lethal weather of hell and climate collapse. In the window boxes of wooden chalets, whose underground concrete garages were stacked with glinting black cars, were shivering geraniums shaking their hot-pink blossoms at the winter sun. I thought of the writing on the wall at Belshazzar's feast.

Almost everyone here, I was to find, knew about the twin emergencies of climate and, to an extent, of nature collapse. Interestingly, they felt compelled to show us they knew. What they didn't seem to know about are feedback-loops, such as the melting of the Arctic sea-ice and the release of permafrost methane, which mean we are on a one-way trip to horror in destabilising not only climate but rainfall, farming and therefore civilisation itself. And even if they *knew* we were in trouble, they didn't seem to *feel* it—they weren't scared, perhaps because no-one else was scared. They *were* like sheep, accepting their cues from the flock.

Denial is interesting. Many of the people of power are well intentioned. And many of them have children. And yet their behaviour and their parenthood don't connect. While they could be hugging their children for what may, if they have anything to do with it, be one last time, many are conspiring, directly or indirectly, to thwart the plugging of the wells instead.

There is talk of change further down the line—but a sufficiently rapid decarbonisation to save us is envisaged by hardly anyone here, barring us. Their standard milestones—2030, 2050, 2070—are too late. For all we know 2025 is too. And besides, it is not milestones but carbon budgets which give us the best clue to the horrors which, having already come for some, await the rest of us.

The denizens of Davos had no sense of emergency. Given the science, their faces should have resembled a Munch or a Bacon and yet, in the pavilions of successive multinationals scattered around the village, converting Davos itself into a fading map of expiring power—in my hearing at least, not one person screamed.

With a friend and XR colleague I stormed the Facebook pavilion and asked to be heard. And—we were heard, in a corridor buffeted by human traffic, by someone unexpectedly receptive and unexpectedly senior who, having left two small children back home, couldn't tear themselves away. Facebook symbolised the new media. If someone with an atomic weapon needs several big red keys to be turned simultaneously to destroy a universe, we also need keys to save one, and both Facebook and Google must be converted into big green keys. Which will be hard, because Facebook and Google's business model *is* high-carbon advertising.

I was also asked, unexpectedly, to address a massive dinner of the global powerful—mainly those amongst them inclined to recognise there was a serious problem, but still not acknowledging the problem as the live emergency it is. I remembered Arnold Schwarzenegger playing the Governor of California, i.e. himself, in the movie *2012* and announcing on the television news that everything is fine, just as the roof caves in, squishing him. As I rose to speak, the powerful fell silent, their hands on the bases of wine glasses which some of them rotated, and I said, rather rapidly—

This is quite unexpected and I'm lost for words.

But then I asked them why, given what we know, *they* weren't all screaming. This is a theme of mine—denial. We are, as I like to put it, in denial about denial—it is such a potent enabler of misery and evil. I reminded them of that celebrated psychological experiment where someone is filling out a form to apply for a job, and smoke starts billowing from under a table. The other applicants are actors and ignore it. The job applicant looks at them, looks at the smoke, and goes on filling out her form. We are that someone, I told them, assiduously filling out our application forms whilst our children roast.

The world has already warmed by over a degree and we don't like what we see—floods, hurricanes, fires, millions of deaths from hunger and conflict. It is warming still and we are entering a terrain where, because of tipping points and positive feedback loops, what we do or don't do won't matter. The world will go on warming regardless until, like a feverish patient, it has killed the microbes sickening it. I said that no society which is willing to harm its own children deserves to survive, yet ours is making just such a horrific spectacle of itself, gagging to hand them over in exchange for frivolous things like SUVs, cruises, over-heated or over-cooled homes. We sacrifice our children to oil, to cheap energy, to consumerism like there's no tomorrow, and consequently bring no tomorrow about, for them at least.

I reminded them that the leaders of the Warsaw Pact countries and even their inhabitants didn't sense the coming end of their regimes. Even the Davos architectural vernacular—flat-roofed ribbon developments, punctuated by the *belle époque* hotels—sings of a Warsaw Pact spa. And we, I said, don't sense the coming end either. The Warsaw Pact had been systematically destroying value and, by manufacturing stuff less valuable than the damage caused, we were too. Built on the quicksand of the climate and ecological collapse, the regimes under which we live in the West, however steady they seem are, like those of the Warsaw Pact, crumbling from within.

Afterwards, each of the others who were asked to speak, spoke looking at me, or rather at my XR hat, as if what it represented had become the shared conscience of the gathering. And after that they clustered round this hat, just as the peasants had clustered round K. at the beginning of *The Castle*, asking if they could get in touch. There was an electricity— perhaps because at last someone was telling them the truth, moral and material, which can be spiritually soothing, if dangerous.

I call it squeaking truth to power. It's the powerless we must speak it to.

Paradiso

The following day I took a juddering funicular drawn on a spindly matt black wire up the Schatzalp. As I slowly ascended, as in an ancient lozenge-gated lift, I considered those bling-folk, the oligarchs of Davos, and how they too had appeared, like the singed koalas of Snow Rebellion, to be marching in place. I thought of *The Ballad of Reading Gaol*—if the queues they so eagerly joined seemed to be moving forwards, it was only because those who finally arrived at the front and were able to pass through the scanners and go in to one of the hotels, would almost immediately come out again and go round to rejoin the back of the queue. Was I right in my understanding that the queue was the place to be, was the purpose of all this, rather than the ostensible destination, just as the traffic jam is not the by-product but the purpose of the city—to burn oil even while going nowhere? If so, that seemed to model our city lives too, which were all about waiting and not about spirited nourishment. It was true, of course, that only in the queues, with their endless waiting, their materialised FOMO, did you get a chance to fully get to know the CEO ahead of you, or the MAD game-theorist behind.

So, if the koalas had been marching in place, at least they were facing forwards, into an agonising future, with expressions of courage and resolution. The oligarchs in their queues were also marching in place, but many of them were facing backwards in token of denial.

At the top of the funicular, with the village laid out neatly far beneath us, was a solitary nineteenth-century sanatorium perched amongst spruce and firs. It was honeycombed with balconies, of a gay barley-sugar cast, and seemingly unmodernised. I noticed that the toilets, under the main staircase, were not divided according to gender, and were immense, greying behind their doors of frosted glass as if built for a race of giants. They spoke eloquently of the mundane fabric—its scents, its foods, its tastes—of the past. I imagined them in use by Mann's Mme Chauchat (madame hot cat), and even Mann himself. It was on just such a honeycombed façade—reminiscent of a Mississippi paddle steamer shorn of its paddles, adrift on rippled snow, that Mann's hero Hans used to lie on his balcony under a bearskin and take stock—

> 'The highest of the sanatoriums is the Schatzalp–you can't see it from here. They have to bring their bodies down on bob-sleds in the winter, because the roads are blocked.' 'Their bodies? Oh, I see. Imagine!' said Hans Castorp. And suddenly he burst out laughing, a violent, irrepressible laugh, which shook him all over and distorted his face, that was stiff with the cold wind, until it almost hurt. 'On bob-sleds! And you can tell it me just like that, in cold blood! You've certainly got pretty cynical.'

Davos, then, as now, was an asylum for those suffering from consumption.

It was here at the top of the funicular, hidden in a snowy forest beside the honeycombed hotel, that the climate scientists were camping, together with Greta Thunberg and her crew, at what they called *Arctic Basecamp*. Morally and physically lifted above the revellers in Davos below, they tell a story of high responsibility and stubborn resolution. They were launching a campaign, witnessed by only a couple of dozen of us, named *Unite Behind the Science*, calling for those in power to listen at last to the scientists, and even to grant the scientists power, since those who held it at present were flunking, in so decidedly betraying not only the *common good*, but even their own, and above all that of their children. Later we held what we call *Fire Circles* for them—dialogic sharing circles, around a fire burning in the snow—to help them face their fears—and rise to them.

The flunkers of Davos below us, meanwhile, were largely operating, like those Victorian automata which were direct descendants of eighteenth-century *tableaux vivants*, on the self-interested and material plane. The rebels in the snow, far below them in turn but climbing steadily upwards over frozen rocks and cataracts, their faces raised towards their goal, were operating in a mode of high idealism and self-protection. Beneath them again was the plane of the peoples of the world, soon to be definitively flooded along with their bus stations and nuclear reactors, burned along with their forests and homes. They were no more than the audience of this comedy—sleeping through the performance until personally drowned and scorched, if then. Wake up and smell the flesh! And finally, here, far above all three planes and gazing sadly downwards from our mountain ledge, crowded with spruce and firs, are barely two dozen climate scientists and UN big cheeses, together with that modernised Jeanne d'Arc, Greta.

The sleeping populace, the protestors, the oligarchs, the scientists—those, as I see it, are the four planes of Davos. How to set them all moving, marching in place no longer, but striding towards their fates?

While my instinct is to go on climbing, up into the snows and trees. But the trees and my hair are on fire and the snow is molten. Roc x

The Emotional Alphabet Children

> Little girls
> with flaming towns for tiaras
> in earrings of pandemic lamentations
> *Wislawa Szymborska*

Dear Xhjjjkcghkflkioghjsss aka Roc,

Thank you gracias for the long piece about Davos, which needs much decoding, and I'll have to re-reread it, at least in places, but yes, I agree, we can't have everything, we have to choose between different *goods*. Hilarious your idea of the womb as the holy grail. I thought your holy grail was saving the planet! I suppose you were just kidding, unless there's a subplot ... Love your definition of Kafka as 'A maze went in search of a child', hopefully a child's game played in eternity. Shall we keep all of this or cut it out? Your fascination with Kafka (Have you seen *The Trial* by Orson Welles? ... It's excellent ... love Welles, especially *F for Fake*), reminds me there is a story by Borges I wanted to allude to in this dialogue. It's been in the back of my mind for ages. I might have mentioned it to you, fleetingly. As all these pages have happened between other projects, with so many interruptions and cogito interruptus, many ideas are side-lined or forgotten. In *The Immortal*, the immortals build a city so senselessly monstrous, they end up abandoning it, and, immersed in pure thought, start living in caves, as if that was the best of all possible worlds. Becoming troglodytes might not be that appealing to most people, but the story is certainly an ironic indictment of urban space and civilisation as we know it:

> This City ... is so horrific that its mere existence, the mere fact of its having endured—even in the middle of a secret desert—pollutes the past and the future and somehow compromises the stars.

Was so excited and proud to see Blue's book, *Challenge Everything*, published ... So looking forward to reading it ... I bring some good tidings too. As you were toiling on accelerating decarbonisation related to all these companies and institutions, their false accounts, greenwashing and flagrant breaking of the Paris Agreement, I too have been endeavouring on the conundrum, wondering why ask some of our governments and billionaire media to tell the truth, when so many of them are beholden to big polluters. So, yes, it is corporations that we should be addressing foremost, though of course, governments could do so much if the will was there.

As you know, I have this fascination with neuroscience, and though I'm aware of its limitations, the complex relationship between mind and brain, and the issues related to free will, I tend to google 'Neuroscience and ...' ... whatever I'm interested in ... e.g.: the seven deadly sins, money hoarding, the controversial amygdala hijack.. So, in these devastating Covid days of death, strange solitude and a kind of reckoning, thinking that climate crisis casualties are going to be even worse, I wound up googling:

Greed.

Trillions of greed.

The Neuroscience of Greed.

Algorithms of sorrow.

So, it was tears, and bottomless lakes of sadness. Many of us dwell on our planet's breathtaking manifold poetry and beauty, as well as on the millions of lovely humans who are striving to protect it and ensure our own survival as a species, taking pains to partly thwart the horrific movie ahead, and we wonder how anyone wouldn't want to do the right thing ... Then the complex irrationality of it all comes to the foreground, the kaput moral compass: the cheating, the lobbying, the violence and indifference to what happens to the only home we have, and to us, the dwellers, which includes all living creatures. It all points to psychopathy. It signals that the blind spot is empathy. In fact, most of our social, economic, climatic, ecological and psychological woes come from a malfunctioning of the empathy switch: the self/other switch is stuck on self. We have a system stuck on self, though across the globe, millions are shouting we urgently need profound change in mindset, mind-shift, benign shape-shifting. There are barriers of complacency, and barriers of indifference, but the main obstacle is that those with money and power only want to protect their power and their money. While web searching, it dawned on me we need the big polluters, the toxic corporations and their lackeys to agree to intensive treatment, as it is their psychopathic greed that stands in the way of the real, meaningful, urgent change that the emergency and our civilisation require. Of course, that would include the polluters of the mind. Happily, I found lots of people, including many experts, have been dreaming the same dream.

Googling about the subject at hand, there was an intriguing glimmer of hope as I stumbled on *The Emotional Alphabet Children* and their treasure trove of crazy ideas, memes, brandalism and actions designed to highlight the insanity of our society. If apocalypse and volatility marks their future, most of them are on a mission to educate us, while others are even willing to risk their lives for our future. I'm in love with these kids. It is heartening, and touching, and ultimately heart-breaking, that so much courage, light and grit should come from frightened but brave teens from all walks of life, but of course, they know what the tense future holds. They're entreating us to act fast, and, with Greta, they're saying: 'How dare you?' And: 'Don't come to us for hope'. Because brave, ardent and dogged as they are, they're also spoken by helplessness, and like so many adults, also suffer from day and night terrors where their bodies are paralysed by the climate and nature emergency incubus. They say they're just a voice in a continuum of voices, but these intrepid kids are always boots on the ground of climate crime scenes, deeply aware of the hellscape, and that most of the crises that plague our lives are interconnected. Ominously, they receive death threats, their laptops are confiscated by the police regularly, and sometimes, their homes are searched. I was thrilled to discover they were liaising with neuroscience researchers, clinicians, trick cyclists, shrinks, behavioural researchers, mycologists, and philanthropists, some of whom are really young, as part of a project called ROMA, which stands for 'radix omnium malorum avaritia': Greed is the root of evil.

It was The Emotional Alphabet Children that realised there were telling gaps in the movement.

To be heroes and heroines every Friday.

Not all children and teen activists can do so, not if they want to fly largely under the public radar.

The big polluters have names and addresses. The Emotional Alphabet Children hacked a large stash of related personal contacts and invited their super-privileged children and grandchildren, who live in $5.5-million hell holes, to come out and play. The inkling was that they'd be profoundly ashamed about their folks' relentless role in wreaking havoc with our environment and our prospects as a species. They found most of them shuddering in their daily knowledge that their folks are sick and sickening, though some, undoubtedly brought up by climate deniers, had muddled views. Horribly, they're part of their dubious world.

Realising that the battle for the future of our species is inextricably linked with treating these kids' folks, that's to say, corporate psychopathy, The Emotional Alphabet Children invited them to the planetary alarm cafe and sent them on an impossible task, as if from a fairy tale. So, within the movement, there is now this 'secret' cabal of millennials who happen to be the children and grandchildren of billionaire psychopathic corporate CEOs and/or their accomplices. They're known as the kids of Carbon City et al. I believe some of them are now secretly active within XR, but their work mainly takes place in the shadows of their families, largely propelled and inspired by wild suggestions whispered by The Emotional Alphabet Children: 'Play, fool around with the lethal parasites,' they say.

The kids of Carbon City et al have begun to play seriously.

Knowing their main inheritance is a black box, and soul-destroyingly seeing themselves as the doomed offspring of serial planet killers, they're now on the special mission they've been called for. Having first-hand knowledge of how lacking in empathy their folks are, when it comes to the planet and all living things, they catch daily glimpses of their folks hooked, as if they were zombie junkies, to greater and greater money-lust shots, which keep on destroying the only home we have. With all the science about the climate and biodiversity crisis out in the open for anyone to find out, these kids are putting all their endeavours in seeking psychopharmacotherapy for their dangerously deranged families, for the sake of their loved ones and that of the planet as we know it. You see, their fairy-tale mission is to persuade their folks to undergo treatment and stop the fatal harm. Some, seeing themselves as planting seeds of sense, are pouring their fortunes into ROMA, or else stealing their parents' credit cards and, knowing they won't notice, donating exorbitant amounts to their pet causes. Others are Hikikomori developing apps to crash fossil fuel stocks. Luckily, I talked to some of them, and now I'm waiting to hear from some of the relevant neuroscientists, with whom I'll be working.

Sky, who's planning to do a degree on neuroscience, petite, blond, braces, fiercely sensitive and intelligent, refuses clinical pessimism regarding received ideas that psychopathy can't be treated. We spoke on Facetime. She was sipping what looked like carrot juice, and kept twirling her hair. 'As children, grandchildren and nieces of corporate psychos, we are their Achilles' heel,' she said. 'Callous as they are, our psychos love us in their own way. We know they have a deep need to be loved and cared for. Somewhere deep down they know they're shit, and are dissatisfied with their thuggish anti-social behaviour. They want to be loved, and we hate them, and love them too. When my dad looks in the mirror while shaving, there's no one there, honest. He tried to hide his loathsome nature but my mum got fed up with the prostitutes, his ruthless sensation-seeking, his weaknesses. He was devastated when she left him. Together with experts, we are working on the dark triad. Machiavellianism, psychopathy, and narcissism. In relationship to climate change, and sustainable entrepreneurship. Well, we're working on the dark tetrad, really, as sadism seems to be part of the problem too. Would you let a blind person fly a plane? That's what's happening with some of our reckless folks, the bloody planet-wrecking CEOs who are bloody throwing all this blood money into bloody planet-wrecking investments. We have limited access to their stone hearts, but access after all.'

'It's well known that corporate psychos comprise the greatest threat to humanity, the planet ... and ha, global business ethics. True, ethics isn't their forte. Psychopathy exists on a spectrum. Is there a Machiavellism test?' I asked.

'Yes, there is. Actions spell out the Machiavellic mind,' she said, watching me with curiosity, as if I was a nearly extinct animal. And added: 'I've meticulously researched the neurobiology of the corporate malaise ... My dad needs his 'money high' at least five times a day. He's just like the godawful junkie who'd kill a granny to get his next shot, but of course, he's getting his 'killings' on a planetary level. The stakes need to be higher and higher. Money acts on the brain's reward system. It increases dopamine, which gives you a feeling of internal euphoria. It increases testosterone. Of course, women have testosterone too! Money, power, control! We all cringe at his grandiose sense of self-worth and criminal versatility. He sees everyone else as insignificant insects. His words, because of course, there's no such thing as an insignificant insect. When my parents divorced, he continued hooked to trading like there was no tomorrow. The highs, the money, protect him against his dark dogs.'

'Do you mean depression, guilt, anxiety, shame?' I asked.

'Well, yes, he was sorely neglected by his parents, but it's all upended. He's grown a black hole in his brain and heart. He's intensely opportunistic, blind to anything that doesn't bring him greater financial success. I've often seen him showing off and guffawing about buying off politicians and lobbying. He thinks being a bully is cool,' she said.

She suddenly put her hand on her mouth, made a waiting sign and left.

When she came back, she apologised, wiped her face, and said she'd been vomiting. 'Maybe the smoothie I had this morning was off?'

'Oh, sorry ... We can talk some other time,' I said.

'No, I'm OK.'

'OK, so how are you going to get your dad to have treatment?'

For some weird reason, she showed me a Japanese erotic art print of two women during cunnilingus. 'My dad has a vast collection in the basement. All art is erotic,' she said, twirling her blond hair.

I wondered whether she was speaking through an alcoholic reverie and translated my inner giggle into a laconic but bemused: 'And?'

'He tends to visit it twice a week, with a glass of D'Amalfi Limoncello Supreme. I've been painting beautiful pictures of ancient woodlands, pristine rivers and extinct species which were millions of years old, and now and again I hang them in front of his Japanese erotic art collection and tear them up before him. He gets really miffed and mutters: Oh, you dear silly girl! Sometimes, there are a few exchanges of cruel language, and I slam the door. Then, whenever I can, I sneak into his office and change his desktop image and screensavers with devastating pictures of oil spills, the ones his company denies creating, claiming sabotage. You know, pictures of Nigerian farmers from the Niger Delta standing in a river with their hands and legs covered in clumps of crude oil, that kind of thing.'

'Is it working?'

'It's slow progress! It's not easy raising parents the right way. We're trying to understand them, so we can help them. This isn't our main work, but I'm also Whatsapping him selfies followed by pictures of dead wildlife, and broken heart emoticons. He says I'm too young to get it. To get what? That I'm the daughter of a psychopath who's destroying our future? That ecological collapse is my family's nemesis?'

'But these things are just minor annoyances,' I said.

'It's guerrilla warfare. I nudged him to do the Hare's Psychopathy Checklist, so he can get to grips with his lethal mental condition. He got 35 out of 40. He may never be cured, but he can be treated. We're all trying to get through to our psychos. We're also working with some doctor activists so that notorious CEOs, politicians and students of Economics and Business undergo a thorough assessment of where they stand on Hare's Psychopathy Checklist and the Dark Tetrad every six months, and have treatment where necessary. It goes without saying that the recommendation is that they're barred from holding jobs where they endanger the population. You know? You should talk to Marina, she's the one who catalysed us and created the ROMA toolkits.'

I also zoomed with Violet, who had a jungle background, and warrior-like, was wearing an orange band across her forehead.

In spite of a great worried frown, Violet looks like a frivolous posh teenager, but I soon realised that it was just a disguise. I was told she's a fan of the world-famous conservation activist, Jane Goodall, that she's in love with the tree people, and that she's convinced that oil-lust killed her dad, a hedge fund trader, who died of a suspected heart attack in Dubai at the age of 45. Her sisters and mum moved to California, a kind of emotional exile. Her grandparents and uncles have big stakes in dirty business.

'It's the end of our innocence. We have so much unlearning to do,' she said. 'Social murder, climate murder which is social and biodiversity murder, biodiversity murder which is social and climate murder. I'm designing a blood calculator app. It calculates all the blood shed by humans and animals due to lack of empathy.' And then she added: 'We provide intel. We're whistleblowers.' And then she giggled: 'It's so boring during lockdown! I miss the analogue world! For fun, every so often, when there's no one around, we also turn the surveillance cameras off and throw red paint on the impeccable façades of our homes. We take pictures and send them to the press with fake names. It's one of the rules. Ours is a quiet rebellion.'

I grinned and wondered out aloud:

'Rules?'

'We've set ourselves some morally-uplifting-mischief rules. That's one. Another one is to conjure up digital ghosts, and subverts which pop up when our folks are checking oil stocks and ... other sabotage operations. Some of us are helping to kickstart Corporate Psychopaths Anonymous, pretty much based on the 12-step programme, but with spirituality based on nature and magic mushrooms. Will be regularly flooding their inboxes with invites to join.'

'Did you say magic mushrooms?'

'Yep, I don't know enough about it. Something to do with oceanic feelings and the infinite abyss of human suffering. For fun, we're also putting stickers in their office toilets that read BE PART OF THE F*****G SOLUTION, NOT THE F*****G PROBLEM. And sending them messages with broken heart emoticons saying CLEAN UP! RESIGN! SIDE WITH THE PLANET! I know they sound like clichés, but, well, we've triggered a few resignations. They just see us as spoilt kids following what they say is just a fashion, but we can see a bit of them crumbling inside.'

'Sometimes it must feel like you're hitting your head against a wall.'

'Some walls are porous, but some of our billionaire folk are pretty intractable and unapproachable. I know the trick is to not get stuck in the doomsday portal, but I've been smelling the acrid smoke of the burnt down trees and singed wildlife for months ... It's all ash. And now we have all these power cuts due to unprecedented Arctic weather. Both probably harbingers of the future ... It's unforgivable.'

Violet started crying.

When we hung up, I cried too.

That night, I dreamt about a suffering calculator and a red tree of life.

It was only recently that I managed to talk to seaweed-hair Marina, whose piercing eyes are fiery green. She was surrounded by the ancient forest empathy posters that will audaciously supplant ads in bus stops all over the country, and was wearing a large word earring.

Her voice was soft but laced with spirit, and a Welsh accent.

'Let's face it. We have a system that rewards ugliness. A system which rewards and encourages unethical growth and whose GDP is largely based on destruction and extermination is a psychopathic system. A few years ago, I was really into transhumanism ...' she said, opening her eyes to their widest extent. 'Then, during the rebellions, I had a lightbulb moment while looking at the pink XR banners that read out EMPATHY. I realised the magic word is empathy, which is self-transcendence, which is ultimately self-preservation. That moment led me to start ROMA, contact the Social Psychology and Neuroscience Lab, and hack the billionaire kids' mobile numbers.'

'"Self" is usually the default mode, but most of us can make the switch to other-oriented behaviour.'

'Exactly. The pandemic's been screaming about empathy as the key to survival. It's inspired a conversation about it. And the unexpected outcome of this shit, fucked, exhausting, long nightmare is that as researchers raced for a Covid vaccine, those working on social neuroscience tuned into further research on empathy as a way of averting social, climate and ecological chaos. Empathy and action, you walk the talk. We got in touch with them.'

'Averting? What about adapting too? But, yes, we need mitigation to avert the worst, and profound action ... I hear there's a lack of studies in neural communication in psychopathic personalities, that further investment and research on effective interventions to target psychopathic greed ...?'

'ROMA now has hundreds of volunteers of all ages, backgrounds and nationalities working on funding and general mind-shifting, lobbying for earning limits, demanding a cornucopia of green jobs, because people need to feel safe economically. Of course, we need more volunteers. It's a Herculean task. As to treatment, there's cool news. There's hope for transcranial direct current stimulation. Neural networks can be modulated. And they're also working on a chip that replaces dead empathy circuits, makes dormant empathy circuits spring into action, and specifically targets different degrees of dispositional empathy. Funnily enough the implant they're working on will be called Ultima™ ... And guess what? We've managed to get some ecocidal CEOs to come forward for the first trials ... Sky's dad is part of the first trials. Yet again, we need to break through the blithe indifference and get more corporate psychos on board.'

I experienced her words as a sweet caress.

'Hey, well done! This world could be so beautiful.'

'And we're now working on the children of the judiciary. And the children of those who follow orders. It also has an effect on empathy neural paths. And we'll be working on the spineless. Neuroscientists should definitively work on an anti-spinelessness chip too ...'

A flick of her head, and the wooden rounded words in her earring became legible:

EAT THE RICH

I laughed and said: 'I'm not sure I like your cannibal earring ...' And: 'Materialism is so last century.' And: 'That sounds ace. The judiciary's crucial to making ecocide law, which is the main way forward ... By the way, I heard you've also been in touch with mycologists? What's that about?'

'Some neuroscientists at Johns Hopkins are fungal evangelists. They're researching different doses of psilocybin mushrooms, as they seem to rewire our brains. Through them I became friends with a mycologist who claims these shrooms enable you to see the view from within a forest, from within a plant, moss, microbe, affording you a sense of ecological oneness, a sense of interconnectedness with all people and creatures accompanied by a sense of sacredness and reverence.'

'It sounds mind-blowing, but I suppose there's also the risk of a bad trip?'

'It depends on the dose. They say a really high dose can make you hear the constant primal scream of suffering. It can make you experience every person and creature currently alive who's suffering. Hellish as it is, the hypothesis is that the experience can activate dormant empathy neural paths. You can imagine where this goes. Some of the billionaires' kids are really into the idea of spiking their folks' drinks, ha. We're pulling out all the stops. We won't stop until the sky is awash with empathy. And empathy multiplies like wild vegetation. And there'll be rivers and endless geographies of empathy and it will erase the devastation and we'll be again dear ocean children.'

Marina walked away so I could see her whole body and started sinuously moving her arms and legs in a slow dance in front of the iPad. She was barefoot, and while dancing, she told me she's oh-so-besotted with one of the tree protectors from HS2 Rebellion, well, with all of them, really, polyamory, but with one of them in particular. Her energy is exhilarating and highly contagious. When the endless lockdowns are over she wants me to forest bathe with her after taking some psilocybin. It'd be beautiful. I told her I'll think about it, though of late, I've learnt not to dip into water unless I know how deep it is, but I'm now part of the ROMA team, always aware of time running out, but always hopeful, behaving and acting as if there's hope, knowing we have to act fast, to incessantly speak truth to power, forever in awe of all those who do so.

September 2020: On Edge, The September Rebellion

We are on edge. Since March 2020, Roc has been isolated on the tiny Hebridean Isle of Gometra. Everything feels upended, courtesy of Covid. Surviving is becoming the new art form. Sadness pervades empty streets and deserted bar terraces, with mourning written in the air, though nature has rebounded in some places in unsuspected ways. As yet, carbon emissions have barely dropped, partly due to the increase in household energy consumption, as well as the factories which continue with their relentless toxic overproduction. In August, Ocean Rebellion was launched, and an Ocean Rebellion armada targeted a mega-polluter, a mega-ship, *The World*, one of many, projecting protest messages on its hull which condemned its dirty activities. A fortnight later, OR's banners and flags, which warn of the death of the oceans, made their first appearance in Parliament Square. 5th September was a day of jubilation. It became No Murdoch Trash day as five major national newspapers, which fail to tell the truth, and stoke hatred, went missing from some newsagents' shelves, after members of XR blockaded two UK printworks owned by Rupert Murdoch's News Corp, with beautifully ingenious bamboo tensegrity structures.

Now autumn leaves are about to fall. And we are already falling. And we are scrambling to get up. With Covid dominating the news, and almost erasing the climate and biodiversity emergencies, which are the overriding existential mega-threats, the September 2020 Rebellion saw all of us rebels wearing masks, socially distanced in a sunny Parliament Square. Not having taken public transport since before lockdown, I whizzed there with my e-bike, and when locking it, I was astonished to see an intrepid but responsible snail in the front basket. A snail with a mission. Resolute, like all of us, to take part in protesting for life, it must have enjoyed the exhilarating ride. With a guerrilla gardener, Hugo, I released it in a quiet patch of grass, just as John Lynes, aged 92, was arrested.

There were speeches about the new Climate and Ecological Emergency Bill by doctors and lawyers. There were scientists wearing lab coats. When leaving, knowing that some of these rebels are under physical and digital surveillance, I looked at the streets painted with facts about extinction, and seeing so much police presence, I became distressed with the system so broken, and angrily addressed a few police formations: 'Will you be true to yourself? Some US police demonstrated with George Floyd Black Lives Matter protests, you could be supporting XR.' That night, I was visited by a good omen, a dream. We are waking from a long hibernation, finally emerging from the pandemic. It is a luminous, crispy cold day. A salvo pierces the air announcing renewal. A young girl does a cartwheel across the expanse of a vacant lot. Another one walks from a corner into the scene. And is that Greta Thunberg, coming closer, looking a little bit older and smiling? I think it is, yes. It is the arrival of spring: energy, youth, oxygen, joy, promise, rebellion. We are back.

And then, there was the impressive, wonderfully effective evening organised by Writers Rebel with some of the UK's top activists, actors, journalists and writers talking in the intermittent rain about the dark work of the lobbyists. Gail Bradbrook, one of the co-founders of XR, gave The Money Rebellion Talk. The location was 55 Tufton Street, a factory of climate change denial, the ground zero of lies on the climate, where thinktanks tell our government what to do and manufacture the reality the BBC broadcasts. The liquid event ended with the stencilling of LIES, LIES, LIES and pouring blood on the steps of 55 Tufton Street, courtesy of Clare Farrell, Jessica Townsend and Rupert Read who were proudly arrested, but not charged, as we sang 'People Have the Power'.

It was electrifying. As I cycled back home in the drizzle, I thought of the last times I'd heard this song sung by rebels. And I thought of much-loved, twenty-five-year-old wildlife biologist XR activist 'Iggy' Fox, who tragically left us on 6 February 2020 while taking part in anti-poaching training in South Africa, an inexplicable loss and an example of how you choose to be in the world. I remembered his love, courage, intelligence and passionate actions. The shock reverberated through many of us. When this saddest of events happened, there was a pause at the centre of the being of XR. His inspirational mother, Liz Jensen, a climate writer and rebel, wrote a piercingly beautiful letter addressed to him. Retrospectively, I dedicated 'Trafalgar Sq Rhapsody' to him, as I'd started writing it two days before his passing, and had been looking at the pictures of his arrest during the October Rebellion, thinking of sharing them with him. Roc said he'd be remembered as the Che Guevara of XR. With XR Youth and other rebels, he fervently vandalised the Brazilian Embassy with a chaos of red paint, red handprints and stencilled slogans that screamed about Brazil's government's blood-soaked hands and ongoing destruction of the lungs of the planet: FOR THE WILD ... NO MORE INDIGENOUS BLOOD ... MAKE ECOCIDE LAW. His life was inspiring on many fronts: as part of the XR Media team, as a relentless fighter for Indigenous rights and wildlife, as a science communicator and writer who knew, and acted, rather than becoming a mere scribe of the apocalypse. His magnificent wake on 13 February in Trafalgar Square was an impassioned and sad reminder of what is possible.

The true value of life is life. To protect it, to make better, to make a difference.

But how to make corporations shed their destructive skins? How to break the trance? How to react to new climate-wrecking ventures that are oblivious to self-extermination? How to make these savages wake up from the anarchic drive to power which dismisses mass-murder of all life as mere collateral damage? How to make them use their neocortex instead of their greed-hijacked brain which only sees the immediate reward? We urgently need a cure for murderous avarice and lack of evolutionary intelligence. The old patriarchal structures, with their amoral corruption, equal mass death. We have to ceaselessly seek for ways to break their lethal inertia. With Covid, we have learnt we can self-sacrifice for our own good and the good of others. We are not basically selfish, that is another pernicious myth. We cannot afford to become numb to this crisis of crises. The frenzy of the now has to morph into the frenzy of Act Now. Pathological selfishness has to be replaced by urgent care. Hope has to become vigilant, while constellating and celebrating the positive twists and turns, and sudden narrative swings in this horror story of human-driven catastrophe. At long last, the nightmarish racist, fascist, sexist, delusional psychopath, who also happens to be one of the most dangerous climate deniers, has exited the White House, giving way to a government which promises to move forward climate change priorities; some countries, cities and institutions are now coming up with initiatives to divest from oil, stop oil production, as well as measures to prevent environmental harm; the untimely passing of nine-year-old Ella Kissi-Debrah, who had severe asthma, has resulted in the first ruling of air pollution as a cause of death, a landmark case; an international team of lawyers are forging a legal definition of ecocide; and there are countless acts by NGOs, as well as thousands of individuals, which are leading to good outcomes, fostering an inspiring sense of collective possibility, and elevation about self-sacrifice. Like those trailblazers who ceaselessly work to benefit present and future lives, we have to envision ourselves as agents of the present and the future of all life. We have to re-enchant ourselves. We have everything to gain with our acts as well as with civil disobedience that will lead to mitigating actions. We need to conjure up a courageous judiciary. We need to forge the willingness to discard the old maps and create a new art of cartography, where the names and locations of these countries, cities, institutions, initiatives, collectives and individuals glint with the scintillating power of true progress on a map of courage. And we need to keep buoyant and true to ensure this map coincides point for point with the whole planet.

2024 Coda

On Tuesday 26 March 2024, at 21:35, rocsandford@xr.earth wrote:

Dear Susana,

Glad we're almost there. Things have changed so much—or haven't—since we wrote this that I've written an afterword to bring it closer to the present,

Roc x

Afterword

Everything's in danger. And everyone. Even the oil & gas folk, who've chosen the life-betraying fork of the prisoners' dilemma and so condemned all of us, themselves too, to repulsive horror. Even what we think we own outright is in danger—our honesty, our kindness, our mortgage.

We'll fall into the power of those who hate us. We'll watch cruelty to people we love. Many of us will indulge in what we once saw as the most intense evil, eating our pets raw, or murdering little girls and boys to quench our thirst.

We may even regret once having roused ourselves from torpor only to attack those who tried to save us, learning first hand that as Kertèsz teaches, Auschwitz is all around us, and inside each of us too. Don't hold your breath, but even if we do earn a little self-knowledge, it'll be worthless beside its cost. Should we choose to fight rather than cooperate, it still won't save us. Not even cooperating will.

Or, alternatively, we can give up trashing nature, consuming propaganda, merrily voting for psychopaths, and buying things made from plastics, or burning oil & gas. Then we can come out on the streets to join our betters. Because what's on offer is to inflate into the fullest possibility of our spirits and bodies—to show what a miracle a human can be.

What's being decided is whether we'll accept that offer, and whether, if we do, it will

be enough to capsize the nasties—the oil & gas folk, the frequent flyers, the slavery-backing fish-eaters—and save what's left.

Roc Sandford, Gometra, March 2024

Addendum

Susana's Postscript: From Writing Rebellion, with Love, June 2021

Rebellion cannot exist without a strange form of love. *Albert Camus*

On Tuesday, 10 August 2021, at 14:55, Susana Medina susanamedina@xr.earth wrote:

Roc

Tempus fugit, doesn't it? Sorry for slight delay in replying. One thing led to another ... Wound up writing this article, an overview of what some rebel writers and artists are up to ... Me thinks we should end the dialogue with it, as an archival homage to them. And also because it adds an extra layer, and caresses the detail on biodiversity loss, something we could have written about at length. What do you think? Or shall we end it with something more elevating, something like a utopian story where grace becomes contagious? With a mesmerising climatic disintegration of everything? Or else, with some black pages?

The IPPC Climate report came out yesterday ... Just downloaded it ... Amazingly, it doesn't mention the words 'fossil fuels', but the knowledge of how terrifying it is, it's now out there. Confirms what was already known years ago: We are facing the biggest fuckup ever ... At least it was on front pages ... for one day ... See you at the Impossible Rebellion! Here my article ... Sxxx

From Writing Rebellion with Love

Do you love the world? Do you love the planet, nature, yourself, or future generations? As an answer to world problems, the word 'love' has vanished from public discourse. It is a word that makes some people cringe as if it had become an embarrassing cliché, a breezy platitude when it comes to dealing with dark times, a truism. Humanity is not that good at love, love is an unsophisticated concept, some people might argue.

And yet, it is the word that some rebel writers keep on repeating, and it has never sounded less corny, fluffy, or vague. They know that love is humanity at its best. Love is depth. Love is hope in action and the opposite of denial. Love is the keyword, the abracadabra that will save us from ourselves. We now have the challenge of challenges, a global emergency: climate breakdown and extinction are already here, and without action, the future of the planet, and its dwellers, will be burning at the stake. We are Code Red. We urgently need global change at all levels: individual, communities, business, institutions and governments. We need the sustainable infrastructure to support cutting emissions. In an unspeakable betrayal, our governments and the billionaire media have been flooding us with lies, and continue to fail us. In the UK, high-carbon and nature-annihilating projects, such as HS2, airport expansion, road development schemes, the bailing out of airlines and the monstrous subsidising of fossil fuels are going ahead in staggering cognitive dissonance greenwashed with empty promises. There are multiple causes which call for global civil disobedience, most of which are interconnected. In *Why Rebel*, writer and environmental activist Jay Griffiths speaks about our moral imagination faltering, and the fact that 'Every shred of mental energy' has to be 'requisitioned for love, essentially the love of life.' She also mentions 'The powerlessness we might feel as writers before the magnitude of such crisis,' while giving us the much-quoted antidote: 'Only when it is dark enough can you see the stars, and they are now lining up to write rebellion across the skies.'

With each rebellion there is a luscious explosion of colour and creativity, the carnival arts, performance and light projections of slogans on guilty façades taking pride of place. Rebellions joyously embrace a wide range of arts, encouraging us to rewild our culture. In times of emergency, rebel writers write short pieces, poems, tweets, Facebook posts, press releases, court defence statements, and sometimes, banners. Some rebels are able to undertake larger projects. *This Is Not A Drill: An Extinction Rebellion Handbook*, which was published in August 2019, contained a declaration of rebellion and twenty-nine essays by highly committed rebels on the need to act now, illustrated with the XR trademark design by the Arts Factory. Some key figures of XR swiftly brought out books: Roger Hallam published *Common Sense for the 21st Century: Only Nonviolent Rebellion Can Now Stop Climate Breakdown and Social Collapse*, on its cover the mural attributed to Banksy, which appeared on a wall in Marble Arch at the end of the April Rebellion, depicting a girl holding the XR symbol by a freshly planted sapling, with the caption: 'From this moment despair ends and tactics begin'; Rupert Read and Samuel Alexander published *Extinction Rebellion: Insights from the Inside* in 2020, while seventeen-year-old Blue Sandford published *Challenge Everything: An Extinction Rebellion Youth Guide to Saving the Planet*. Writers Rebel held its first event on 11 October 2019 with their renowned '40 Top Writers Marathon', continued to create high-profile events such as '55 Tufton Street', and has a frenzied online presence. Many creative rebels who took to the streets during the Extinction Rebellion protests translated the experience into writing, and art, though very few were able to put aside other projects and commitments to only write the rebellion, shaping the experience in a literary book, or to embark on large-scale art projects such as those of artist-activists Ackroyd & Harvey at Tate Modern and the Thames.

Writing and publishing are slow endeavours. Jay Griffiths responded pronto to writing rebellion. Climate change novelist and relentless direct action activist Sue Hampton quickly adapted her experience with Extinction Rebellion 2018-19 into a novel called FOR LIFE, released as an e-book, which I was too busy rebelling to read at the time. This year, she published *Rebelling for Life*, a compilation of short stories, poems, and blogs arranged in a non-chronological way, where she focuses on rebellion, climate grief, and activism against the arms trade. Largely written in a have-been-there direct style, the emotional tone is fiercely honest and the emphasis is on the love that matters: '*agape*, the kind God would feel for humanity, if God existed' as a uni student rebel spending a transformative night in a cell reflects in 'The Prisoner'.

Beginning with an interview where Hampton talks about the climate emergency 'as a knowledge that can't be unfelt or unknown' which shook her to the core, morphing her self-styled keyboard warrior identity into one which embraced non-violent civil disobedience, most of the pieces deal with the emotional reality of being a rebel, the grandma activist being a recurrent theme, which reminds us there is an intergenerational commitment to rebellion. A rebel grandmother herself, Hampton pens 'For Nathaniel', a poem for an action by XR Grandparents and Elders: 'I am here for you/because I'm Grandma/and you, firefly boy, are a spirit to power me', and references XR co-founder Gail Bradbrook in 'Climate Vigil': 'All the children are our children.' In 'Views of an Extremist Grandma', written after rebels were classed as extremists by the police anti-terrorist group Prevent, she sets out her ethics in ten impeccable points which go from accepting the scientific consensus about the climate and ecological emergency, to rejecting war, violence, and divisive ideas about humanity, to the conviction that only non-violent mass disobedience will solve the existential nightmare we find ourselves in. In 'The Activist', #ReggaeGran #NoFrackingNoCrime, who has gained Twitter glory, protests outside ExCel to stop the Arms Fair, and ends up going on hunger strike outside the Yemeni Embassy for twenty-six days: she is 'hungry for peace'.

The first short story, 'The Trial', begins with a district judge in denial, who complains to his unsympathetic wife: 'You've no idea how wearisome these trials are ... I don't care as long as I'm spared the speeches ...', whilst the prosecution lawyer, also at odds with his partner when it comes to XR court cases, is portrayed as someone who 'didn't normally pay attention to the defendants' last-ditch attempts to cram in as much death and doom as possible.' Seen from multiple points of view with contrasting characters, the story narrates the court case of a nineteen-year-old rebel on trial who has decided to defend herself by endlessly repeating: 'This is a climate emergency.' Her mother disagrees with XR methods, while the father finds it unbelievable that rebels like his daughter should be criminalised, seeing the substantial fine as designed to punish liberal parents. Like many who have postponed studying to protest climate inaction, the young rebel announces she'll be leaving uni for as long as it takes.

If in 'Rebelling in Red', Hampton joins The Red Rebels and finds it a 'creative, mysterious way of rebelling: a graceful, emotive and spiritual alternative to blocking roads', in 'Stop the Press', a statement written in a police cell, she does not mince her words when defending the blockade of the printing press with bamboo lock-ons which prevented the distribution of Murdoch's News Corp's newspapers including the *Sun* and the *Times*, as well as the *Daily Telegraph*, the *Daily Mail* and the *Evening Standard*. The media barons who profit from *business as usual* are seen as a 'malignant oligarchy that sets the BBC News agenda and that of most other UK channels', and the action, news of which sparked a day of collective joy in many a quarter, as 'an attempt to highlight the role of five billionaires in a conspiracy to lie and to mislead the British people, thus preventing the change that's so urgent and essential if we are to survive.' In a poem of the same title, she writes: 'For just one day/the lies are stalled.'

Hampton 'tells the truth', for 'the new beginning is a fine root through rubble.' All the pieces in this collection have genre, date, and sometimes location or a brief explanation written at the top, performing as exhibits before a hypothetical trial on her actions when faced with the global emergency. Her depression, like that of many people across the globe, is called 'climate grief': 'The pills can't screen it off and the CBT's N/A.' Love, which is the leitmotif running through the collection, is offered as prerequisite and solution to our climate and ecological woes: 'If protecting life on earth is not what love requires of us, I don't know what is … If we're to change the future we can't delude ourselves. And in a theoretical way I know how to do that without the limiting self-absorption of depression. The secret, as always, is love.'

Rebelling for Life gives us a compelling emotional palate of the world of rebels and peace activists, the seers and deniers, and those affected by their actions, or inaction. The grief, the emotional investment, the depression, the hope beyond belief, the doubts about the efficacy of protest, or being rational and well-behaved when 'weeping and wailing would be more proportionate', the shock at being perceived as a threat to society or ignored, when 'there's the scientific consensus, and the consensus that our leaders are the criminals.' Reading its pages, the mind shifts from the moving serenity and elegiac tone of some of the poems to the sheer clarity, bareness and sometimes, softness of her prose, to the contrasting, chilling effect of her statements, which pre-empt complacency, to counterpoints where playfulness and hope come to the foreground. Thus in 'Kit List', she makes an inventory of what a rebel needs to pack. Amongst the numerous items and qualities, we find: superglue, thermals or sunblock, waterproofs, bust card, a message scribed bold on frayed flat card, a book, high heart and thick skin, facts, tears deep, and all the love you can find.

We are in the age of great dying. The climate and ecological emergency are intimately interwoven, and should be tackled together. If Sue Hampton's pieces deal primarily with the human side of being a rebel, an activist or a nature-loving person, Jay Griffiths' tour de force in *Why Rebel?* makes us highly attuned to the bewildering beauty of the natural world and the soul-destroying biodiversity emergency. 'I wish that everyone who said they believed in angels would actually believe in insects', starts the poignant introduction, a first line that made me smile, gasp and want to continue reading straight away.

Not being acquainted with Griffiths' feral writing, I soon became disoriented, though, as in the first essay she detours to the Futurist poet Marinetti to speak about the ugliness of current politics. A gathering of erudite literary essays from different times, which blend poetry, cultural history, politics, anthropology, mysticism and environmentalism with the personal, Griffiths makes the case for rebellion through a series of loosely connected and fragmentary arguments that range from fascism and 1930s futurism to decry Libertarianism, the Alt-Right, Trump, Bolsonaro and Johnson; shamanism and poetry as healing forces, which have been expelled by the totalitarian state of mind of utilitarianism, efficiency and profit-motives; the nourishing beauty of the soil and the surreally expensive fascination with colonising space when we have a global emergency; Brexit, and a love of land where 'the territory of English indigeneity was stolen by the far right', the real 'Indigenous people' being the protestors who protect the land. These are some of the ideas Griffiths explores. Her fury is commendable, as she condemns the story of the British Empire, which is one of murdering, enslaving, and uprooting Indigenous people, continuing these days under the guise of corporate colonialism, and rails about our self-wounding relationship to nature, our necrophiliac economy and 'the devastating stupidity of it all'.

Although different essays deal passionately with the multi-fanged predicament we find ourselves in, it was when I began reading the pieces on animals, insects and soil that the sheer power, joy, rage and sorrow of this book began to unfold. If 'The Forests of the Mind' is a paean to poetry and metaphor, and a diatribe against the disease of literalism, where she feels 'the fire of pure fury' when it comes to 'the trenchant stupidity of deforestation', in 'Happiness, Animals and the Honeyguide Rule' she invokes the bird called the honeyguide, which 'needs human hands to break open the hive, while humans need the bird to guide them to the right tree'—a lesson about the best relationship between human and 'the more-than-human-world'. Then she waxes lyrical about the joy and tenderness of communicating with animals, inter-mindedness and the unbuyable delight we draw from interspecies community. Having enchanted the reader, she proceeds to condemn species narcissism, and our disregard for irreplaceable habitats: 'The philosophy of human exceptionalism, that arrogant and ultimately self-injurious idea that humans are a species both separate and superior, reaches its apogee in mass extinctions.' Wildlife populations have fallen 68 per cent since 1970; 90 per cent of the Monarch butterfly population has disappeared across the USA; bleaching will kill most of the world's coral within thirty years, and with it, the wider life dependent on it; swallows, martins, nightingales, the number of species undergoing extinction or endangered is gut-wrenching; 'the deadened oceans are an analogy for a wasteland of human imagination.' 'We collectively commit a bureaucratic slaughter that beggars genocide.'

As we face a tsunami of extinctions, Griffiths reminds us that animals and insects are our guides and healers, and a gigantic collective of goodness, in pages that are the most moving you are likely to read on the subject. 'The Narcissist and the Firefly' begins with an unforgettable ode to these tiny creatures, where she reminds us they are our unassuming and bashful minders, as they bring *three quarters* of our food into being, remove dead matter, so renewal can take place, and give us flowers and silk. Insects are crucial to the cycle of life. 'No insects, no Mozart. Without beetles, we wouldn't have The Beatles.' Understanding and cherishing the interconnectedness of everything is vital to our well-being. But there is no love in Narcissus. Regretfully, we live in the age of narcissism, and species narcissism. 'And this is the age of the endlings, the very last individuals of their species.' In a few instances, Griffiths conjures the untold sorrow of the sixth mass extinction, with heart-breaking stories of endlings: 'Modernity's life on earth, brief as a firefly, leaves a toxic dark for ever. In the last of nights, the last star put out on Earth, in the horror of annihilation's finality, a last firefly, lonely to its core in a vast wasteland, glows one last time and is gone for good. Perhaps it will be only in that kind of darkness that we could have seen the magnitude of what we have done and all that we have lost: a world, each other, and ourselves.'

Before the weight of world sorrow, a tatty leaflet found itself in Griffiths' hands: 'Never has one little leaflet made such an impression on me. Two words: Extinction and Rebellion'. Extinction Rebellion, with its emphasis on non-violent direct action (NVDA) has given us the power to create media awareness. Interestingly, Griffiths writes about how bureaucratic, dry scientific words and deadly language about our planetary crisis are responsible for failing to communicate the emergency, and how we need heartfelt words and messages—something Extinction Rebellion excels at. Listing a few of the things we may love, and despairing of the biodiversity crisis, she asks us a question: 'Please tell me you understand the immensity of this ... Let me ask you what you love, what makes you happy. Is it a child? Is it your partner? ... And this love, then, this happiness, tell me how it will even exist without the tiniest of beings, the insects, against which we have been so utterly pitiless?'

Though not writing explicitly about rebellion in most of the pieces, the rebel spirit is there throughout, and the medley of essays, most of which are lyrical, flow fully into it, with the last three contrasting pieces of reportage about Extinction Rebellion which close the book. 'A Time of Rebellion' tells us about the electrifying atmosphere of the April Rebellion, the wonders of superglue, and the terrifying numbers of the reality of climate chaos. Giving a brief history of the protest movements XR honours, and a summary of some of its strategies, Griffiths quotes some of its key figures: arrest is 'the classic sacrificial move', 'I've prototyped prison as a campaign strategy,' says Roger Hallam. She speaks about XR's 'indubitable messianic quality' and joins The Red Rebels who 'perform in silence, and through silence they speak'. She cites Daiara Tukano, who spoke on the Pink Boat 'of the earliest Earth protectors: Indigenous peoples. It is they who protect 82 per cent of the world's biodiversity, they who led the resistance to climate chaos, they who are disproportionately affected by it ... More than 1700 environmental activists have been murdered this century, a disproportionate number being Indigenous people.' Arm inside a lock-on-pipe, she speaks of her fear of being injured when released from it by the police, a fear shared by most rebels who lock-on, and of how lucky she is to find a sympathetic officer when discharged from a night in a cell. And if in '55 Tufton Street', home of the climate-denialist Global Warming Policy Foundation, she exposes the ludicrous lack of expertise of its founders and fellow-denialists, in 'Regina vs Me' she presents us with her impeccable, lengthy defence statement where she speaks of the failure of the government and the media to inform the public of the severity of our predicament, and the unmet binding obligation of our government to educate the public about our crisis. Disruption and arrest are the only viable strategy to get the media to report and raise public awareness, thanks to which XR gained massive coverage, thus contributing to the emergency declaration. Witness statements include that of Professor Lewis: 'To criminalise Extinction Rebellion would be, in effect, to penalise an example of good and thoughtful citizenship. It would, in effect, send a message that the minor inconveniences caused by their actions are more important than the most serious threat to life on earth humankind has ever faced.' Citing all the things she's not going to talk about, she summarises her purpose: 'I am here to talk about justice.' Her defence statement touches the judge: notwithstanding a guilty verdict, he speaks his truth in a tribute to rebels.

Seeded with numerous insights, and lessons from Indigenous cultures and peoples, especially from Indigenous Australian Civilisations, *Why Rebel* communicates a sense of wonder and awe before the natural world, of being wonderstruck, of organic love. After reading it, the soil became truly alive, my irrational apprehension of worms replaced with tenderness: 'worms are ... gardeners of delirious fecundity ... the artists of the turning world.' If Griffiths gives us love, she also gives us rage, her power lying in interweaving literary solace with fury at the state of the world.

Piecemeal writing pervades the rebellion, and it isn't necessarily a bad thing. Both *Why Rebel* and *Rebelling for Life* have a restless, patchwork feel, which I fully understand, for what is happening cannot be made into something whole, and there is also a sense of urgency to publish so as to create awareness. As I was tweaking this piece, I went to Tate Modern to see 'On the Shore' by Ackroyd & Harvey, not knowing their giant grass banner would be travelling from the solemn atmosphere of the Turbine Hall to the Thames, where, becoming public art, it floated majestically, before being composted in the evening. From installation, to ceremonial performance, to festive procession which incorporated the audience, to site-specific work, writing was central to this land art piece. Co-founders of Culture Declares Emergency, Ackroyd & Harvey use photosynthesis to grow living grass artworks, and recently created grass photographs depicting portraits of rebels which were accompanied by writers' performed words. For Tate Modern the artists created a lush, 16-metre-long, grass portrait of that essential element in rebellion, the banner, the material, and the crucial natural process it referred to, photosynthesis, fittingly conveying the message, while the words of Booker prize-winning novelist Ben Okri in astonishing fluorescent yellow, which is the colour of grass when prevented from photosynthesising, reminded us of our sacred duty to protect life:

CAN'T YOU HEAR THE FUTURE WEEPING? OUR LOVE MUST SAVE THE WORLD

A mighty emotional ecosystem, 'On the Shore' was a powerfully choreographed multi-disciplinary ritual, which included a cellist, and a squad of strong performers dressed in mourning black who, headed by a dancer, paraded the grass banner to the river, rolled up like an immense sacred scroll. It also included a large crew of rebels, some of them part of Writers Rebel, who struggled to lay the immense grassy banner on the shore and onto the water, a tense action filled with physical exertion, not least that of the artist Dan Harvey, who, as we were leaving, welcomed some inquisitive newcomers to the floating piece: a couple of ducks.

The rebellion was also written in the speeches that followed. Recalling 'Paint the Streets', Writers Rebel launched 'Paint the Land', which called for writers and artists to create work with the landscape about the emergency. And Ben Okri, whose little daughter sang at the end, made an unforgettable speech that touched us all to the core: 'Love is the only economy, the highest economy of life, the most efficient force of civilisation ... Love is the last power that stands between us and extinction. Only love is endless. This is the time we need to show that we are greater than our history. We can be the agents of change.'

We could all hear the past, the present and the future weeping, which is now becoming inconsolable sobbing. Undoubtedly, there will be more literature and art about rebellion. Love for life will feature largely. Love, fear, suffering, indignation, justice, hope and courage will be the main plotlines, transformation their mission. New voices will emerge that move beyond dystopia. As it happens, I've just come across a tweet that calls for these kind of stories: a new rebel group called XR Wordsmiths is on the horizon, referencing Cyberpunk and Steampunk, and kicking off an art movement that envisions a future that has solved the global emergency using current technologies: Solarpunk. And as it happens I have also come across a promising anthology which I'm now reading, *Poetry Rebellion*, edited by nature writer Paul Evans, 2021, which spans 4000 years of poems and prose to rewild the spirit, ranging from Lao Tzu and Chaucer to Silvia Path, Gary Snyder and Helen Mort. The collection is not supposed to be 'just a sanctuary in which to find solace from environmental grief but a manual for psychic resistance in the war against Nature'. Evans, who sees fear of the destructive forces of nature resulting in ecophobia as a chief factor that has led us to where we are, foresees love as the sequel to the grave existential threat we are facing: 'What will emerge from the emergency … will be created by a rewilding of people radicalised not just by climate strikes and extinction protest, but by a fearless urgent love of a Nature which is good, even when it's bad for us.' Love *is* a sophisticated concept: it encompasses wonder, kindness, protection, care, respect, empathy, gratitude, generosity, courage, sacrifice, work, devotion, connection and understanding. Its manifestations can be manifold. In policy-making terms it would entail drastic action, substantial investment, and legislating against ecocide. The multi-faceted tragedy humanity has created has to be solved by humanity. The antidote prescribed by rebel writers is to be rewilded by love, whatever shape it takes.

Acknowledgments

The poem 'Petite Vilaine', which is mentioned at the beginning, was published in *We'll Never Have Paris*, ed. Andrew Gallix, Repeater Books. Excerpts from *Rebel, Rebel, An Emergency Dialogue* have appeared in different forms in the following publications: 'Trafalgar Sq Rhapsody' on Writers Rebel; 'Dear Angelus Novus', 'We Are the Asteroid, We Are the Dinosaurs', 'Rebel, Rebel', and 'From Writing Rebellion, with Love' on 3:*AM Magazine*; 'To Milk a Unicorn' on *Qualm*; 'Rebel, Rebel, An Emergency Dialogue' was published in the anthology *Without Reduction*, *The Happy Hypocrite* issue 12, and broadcast on *Resonance Extra*. 'Trafalgar Sq Rhapsody' was performed by Valerie Antwi, at Estuary Festival, Rebel, 22 May-13th June 2021, curated by artist-activists Ackroyd & Harvey.

Epigraph translations: Relating to Charles Baudelaire and Walter Benjamin, from Walter Benjamin, *Arcades Project*, translated by Howard Eiland and Kevin McLaughlin; Albert Camus, *The Rebel*, translated by Anthony Bower; Jorge Luis Borges, 'On Exactitude in Science', translated by Andrew Hurley; 'A Moment in Troy', Wisława Szymborska, translated by Clare Baranczak and Stanisław Cavanagh; 'Reflections on sin, pain, hope, and the true way', Franz Kafka, translated by Willa and Edwin Muir; all © the translators, publishers and estates.

In 'Trafalgar Sq Rhapsody' the following authors are referred to by their first name: Roc Sandford, Sue Hampton, Monique Roffey, James Miller, Toby Litt, Cath Drake, Liz Jensen, Chloe Aridjis, A.L Kennedy, Jessica Townsend, Margaret Atwood, Simon Schama, Rupert Read and George Monbiot. The XR crew at 2020 WEF Davos comprised Caroline Päkel, Helena Farstad, Daze Aghaji, Mac Macartney, Rupert Read and Adam Woodhall. Finally, special thanks to Clive Russell and Lorna Scott Fox, and to David Collard who kindly invited us to read our work at many of his events. To protect identities from unwelcome interest, we have not named the creative minds and courageous producers behind the beautiful protests we describe, but together with life at large, we are forever in their debt, however short forever is.

www.ingramcontent.com/pod-product-compliance
Lightning Source LLC
Chambersburg PA
CBHW061230070526
44584CB00030B/4061